W9-DIW-362

ESSAYS OLD AND NEW

2

GEORGE MOORE'S MIND AND ART

GEORGE MOORE'S MIND AND ART

A. NORMAN JEFFARES   MILTON CHAIKIN

WILLIAM C. FRIERSON   WILLIAM F. BLISSETT

HERBERT HOWARTH   GRAHAM OWENS

BONAMY DOBRÉE   BRENDAN KENNELLY

GRAHAM HOUGH

Essays edited by
GRAHAM OWENS

BARNES & NOBLE, Inc.
NEW YORK
PUBLISHERS AND BOOKSELLERS SINCE 1873

First published in Great Britain, 1968
by Oliver and Boyd, Ltd
First published in the United States, 1970
by Barnes & Noble, Inc.

ISBN 0 389 03982 9

Printed in Great Britain by
Robert Cunningham and Sons Ltd, Longbank Works, Alva

ACKNOWLEDGMENTS

For permission to quote from the works of George Moore acknowledgments are due to J. C. Medley, Esq. and R. G. Medley, Esq.

Several of the essays in this collection have already been published elsewhere and for permission to reprint them here acknowledgments are due to: A. Norman Jeffares, "A Drama in Muslin", revised and reprinted from *Essays Presented to Amy C. Stock*, ed. R. K. Kaul, by permission of the author and Rajasthan University Press (1965); William C. Frierson, "George Moore Compromised With the Victorians", reprinted from *Trollopian* (now *Nineteenth-Century Fiction*), Vol. I, no. 4 (March 1947), by permission of the Regents of the University of California; W. F. Blissett, "George Moore and Literary Wagnerism", reprinted from *Comparative Literature*, XII (1961), by permission of the author and editor; Graham Hough, "George Moore and the Novel", reprinted from *Image and Experience*, London (1960), by permission of the author, Gerald Duckworth & Co. Ltd., and the University of Nebraska Press.

CONTENTS

INTRODUCTION

A generation after his death, George Moore's literary reputation remains in the doldrums, and, though a great deal has been written on him, there is a dearth of substantial critical evaluation. True, friends and sympathisers – a large number, in spite of Moore's sharp tongue and gift for mockery (John Eglinton, A.E., Joseph Hone, Edouard Dujardin, Barrett Clark, William L. Phelps, James Huneker, William Archer, Jacques-Emil Blanche, Louis Gillet, Mary Hutchinson, Nancy Cunard, Arnold Bennett, Robert Ross, Havelock Ellis . . .) – have written copiously, but mainly at the level of personal anecdote and reminiscence, though Gosse and Desmond MacCarthy went deeper. Of the work of his younger "disciples" – Charles Morgan, Humbert Wolfe, Geraint Goodwin, James Whitall, John Freeman, and David Garnett – only Morgan, in his *Epitaph on George Moore* (1935), has produced a significant study. Many of Moore's contemporaries, of course – Beerbohm, Wilde, Shaw, Chesterton, Wells, Middleton Murry – satirised the man and the artist with varying degrees of savagery. Yeats, Stephen Gwynn, Susan Mitchell, Frank Swinnerton and Malcolm Elwin wrote more seriously, though often heatedly, of his defects. Yet their fury was, more often than not, a personal reaction against some of his more outrageous comments and behaviour. Moore's personality has for too long stood between the critic and his work. The dust of *Hail and Farewell* has long settled and it is time to look at his real achievement.

There is little current material. The definitive bibliography of Moore's work by Edwin Gilcher, of Cherry Plain, N.Y., has not yet been published. Malcolm Brown's *George Moore: a Reconsideration* (1956) remains the sole full-length critical study of Moore's work. Perhaps the most interesting publication is *English Fiction in Transition, 1880-1920*, which includes annotated bibliographies of writings about Moore, edited by Helmut E. Gerber and others at Purdue University.

One phase of Moore's career has been examined in detail – the earliest, where the bulk of the research has been into the influences that shaped his first novels: French Naturalism and Symbolism (Frierson, Farmer, Ferguson, Marie, Collet, Chaikin, Nejdefors-Frisk, Temple, Steward, Cordasco, Noël, Heywood, Jean-Aubrey, Calvin Brown); the Russian novelists (Phelps, Gettmann); Pater and the English Aesthetics (O'Fáolain and Sechler).

Very little analysis is available, however, of Moore's influence on other writers. He founded no school. But in what ways, for example, did he affect the work of Charles Morgan and David Garnett? How great was his impact on the Irish short story, on James Joyce, Frank O'Connor, Liam O'Flaherty, Sean O'Fáolain, Edna O'Brien, and James Plunkett? Did *The Untilled Field* influence *Dubliners* in any significant way? Did *Vain Fortune* have any effect on the shape of *"The Dead?"* Did *The Old Wives' Tale* owe to *A Mummer's Wife* only its original inspiration and its environment? One of the more urgent tasks is a detailed comparison of Moore's experiments in novel technique with those of Ford, James, the Joyce of the *Portrait*, Dorothy Richardson and Virginia Woolf. Moore was the first English novelist to break away from the content, structure, techniques, and style of the Victorian novel: what precisely was his influence on these later experimenters, what was his contribution to novelistic vision? A systematic study is needed of Moore's place as a short story writer; of his autobiographical writings in their various versions (*Confessions, Memoirs of my Dead Life, Hail and Farewell, A Communication to my Friends*, along with *Avowals* and *Conversations in Ebury Street*); of his relationship with Yeats and their influence on each other's writing; of his various styles, method of work, revisions and manner of "recreating" himself. And there is as yet no good collection of his letters. Above all, critics have tended to concentrate largely on the English phases of Moore's career; the focus of critical attention now requires a shift to his Irish period, to the works – it is arguable – in which he felt most at home: *The Untilled Field, The Lake, Hail and Farewell*, and *A Story-Teller's Holiday*.

The commissioned essays in this volume – Milton Chaikin on the early fiction, Herbert Howarth on the Irish period, Graham Owens on the melodic line in narrative, Bonamy Dobrée on the "prose epics" and Brendan Kennelly on the short stories – are designed to fill some of these gaps, or at least to carry the argument a stage further. And in order to provide a representative selection of critical writing on Moore and to cover all the major aspects of his literary career, reprints of essays already in print have also been included: A. Norman Jeffares on *A Drama in Muslin*, William C. Frierson on what he considers his compromise with the Victorians, William F. Blissett on his debt to Wagner, and Graham Hough on his achievement as a novelist.

One final aspect needs to be stressed. Moore had a fanatical passion for revising and spent most of his life reconstructing and rewriting his books. All his collections of short stories (except the last, *Celibate Lives*) and all his novels, with the sole exception of *Mike Fletcher*, were revised at least once; six of them twice; three of them three times; three four times; one (*The Untilled Field*) five times; and one (*Evelyn Innes*) no fewer than six times in all. Many more rewritings took place before the first editions were issued, and many novels were slightly revised versions of books published in magazine form. In the circumstances, it has not been possible to use standard texts throughout; in each essay, therefore, the first mention of a work specifies the particular edition under discussion and, where necessary, its relation to other editions.

GRAHAM OWENS

A. Norman Jeffares

A DRAMA IN MUSLIN[1]

I

George Moore's activities as "Zola's ricochet" in English literature are marked by *A Modern Lover* (1883), *A Mummer's Wife*
(1885) and the pamphlet *Literature at Nurse, or Circulating Morals*
(1885). He wrote exuberantly to Zola, on 16 Aug. 1885, that he
certainly had a great part to play: "I am fighting that Englishmen
may exercise a right which they formerly enjoyed, that of writing
freely and sanely".[2] His battling created opportunities for
naturalism, for greater freedom in subject and style in the English
novel. His first two novels caused something of a sensation in the
early 'eighties, but today Moore is probably best known in
universities and among general readers for *Esther Waters* (1894),
which is the only one of his works now in print, in an American
paperback edition and in the Oxford Novels Series. This novel is
generally taken as marking – perhaps because it is a more considerable achievement than his earlier work – a particular stage in
the development of the English novel.

Discerning readers of Moore probably also know and enjoy
his autobiographies: the *Confessions of a Young Man* (1888) with its
exuberant artist's defiance of orthodoxy and its often undetected
self-mockery; the devastating self-exploration, apparent naïvety
and malice as well as the irresistible prose of *Hail and Farewell*
(1911; 1912; 1914), in the three volumes of which Moore portrayed *his* Dublin, one no less fascinating than that which Joyce
handled in *Ulysses*. They also may know the Turgenev-like
sketches of Irish peasant life in *The Untilled Field* (1903) and the

---

[1] [Revised and reprinted from *Essays Presented to Amy C. Stock*, ed. R. K.
Kaul. Jaipur (Rajasthan University Press) 1965.]

[2] J. Hone, *The Life of George Moore*, London (Gollancz) 1936, p. 114.

discovery[3] of the melodic line in *The Lake* (1905) so skilfully developed in the imaginative story-telling of *The Brook Kerith* (1916) or the rich historical detail of *Héloïse and Abélard* (1921). It is, however, less likely that *A Drama in Muslin* (1886) will be generally known, although this novel is worth reading on several counts. Its study of the late nineteenth century Anglo-Irish social situation is both interesting and unusual. It can be viewed in several ways. Its place in the history of Moore's development as a novelist is important, for in it he develops a more complex theme and treatment than he had handled in his preceding novel, *A Mummer's Wife*. It marks his realisation that he could not keep up the pace of a Zola; as he put it later, the writing of three naturalistic novels was all the human nervous system could bear. Indeed he wrote to his brother Julian, to enlist his aid, to obtain from him impressions of the Irish background for this novel, to ask him to "take a large packet and a good pencil and write me in disconnected phrases the impressions as they struck you". The novel which followed *A Drama in Muslin*, *A Mere Accident* (1887), certainly lost its drive while Moore was exploring the extraordinary character of his friend and fellow landlord, Edward Martyn, the model for the novel's hero, John Norton – a task attempted again in the "John Norton" of *Celibates* (1895) but not brought to perfection until Moore achieved the brilliant – and undisguised – portrait of *Hail and Farewell*. Moore himself thought that he changed as a novelist with the next novel, *Spring Days* (1888): but the change probably came immediately after *A Drama in Muslin*.

To consider the novel not so much in the context of Moore's development but in a larger context is, however, more rewarding for, in writing it, Moore was following in a genre established for the first time in the history of the English novel by Maria Edgeworth's *Castle Rackrent* (1800). This was the first regional novel, and Maria Edgeworth developed her theme in *Ennui* (1807), *The Absentee* (1812) and *Ormond* (1817). She was followed by Lady Morgan and Charles Robert Maturin. The work of these three

---

[3] Perhaps "apparent discovery" would be more accurate, as Malcolm Brown has discovered the germ of it in *Parnell and His Island*, London (Sonnenschein) 1887. See his *George Moore: a Reconsideration*, Seattle (Univ. of Washington Press) 1955, p. 27; also G. Owens, "The Melodic line", in the present volume.

novelists was written from an Ascendancy viewpoint, though all three were highly critical of the state of Ireland, although their subject naturally included the extremes of Irish life. Novels written from a peasant viewpoint followed on the work of these pioneers, and their authors, Carleton, the Banims and Griffin, also dealt with the same extremes, their attitudes being naturally not a little different from those of their predecessors.

What is common to most of these novels about Ireland is the basic stuff of their regional subject: the two Irelands; rulers and ruled; gentry and peasantry; landlords and tenants. One of the things Moore was doing in *A Drama in Muslin* was to contribute, inevitably, his variation on this particular theme. And his contribution, written after the tensions and violence of the Land League period, reminds us that what ultimately resolved the gulf between landlord and tenant was not so much the bloody years between 1916 and 1923 as the Wyndham Land Act of 1903,[4] which spelt out clearly the coming of the end of the great houses in Ireland.

Moore himself was a landlord; he had inherited Moore Hall at the age of eighteen. At first his desire was to go to Paris to become an artist. When his guardians forbade this he lived in London as a man about town on the five hundred pounds a year which was his income from the estate once the mortgages were paid. As soon as he attained his majority he went to Paris. He took no interest in the estate, though he liked the social standing of being a landlord, but in his late twenties he was forcibly made to realise that the great era of the Ascendancy was waning. The Land League was set up in 1879. Evictions and very bad agricultural

---

[4] Yeats realised the likely effect of this act on great houses and estates such as those of Lady Gregory. "Upon a House shaken by the Land Agitation", *Collected Poems*, p. 106, refers to Coole and the prose draft of this poem puts the matter even more clearly: "How should the world gain if this house failed, even though a hundred little houses were the better for it, for here power has gone forth, or lingered, giving energy, precision; it gives to a far people beneficent rule, and still under its roof loving intellect is sweetened by old memories of its descents far off; how should the world be better if the wren's nest flourish and the eagle's house is scattered?" He followed this prose draft of the poem with its final text and continued, "I wrote this poem on hearing the result of reduction of rent made by the courts" . . . adding praise of Coole . . . "here life moves within restraint through gracious forms. Here there has been no compelled labour, no poverty thwarted impulse."

conditions had exasperated the peasants. They were using the new weapons of boycotting, and their "No Rent" campaign was extremely effective. There were shootings of landlords and their agents, and the occupants of the big houses were (as in *A Drama in Muslin*) acutely aware of "the disturbed state of the country". Moore himself had been abruptly forced to read the latest writings on the wall. A letter had come to him in Paris from his uncle, Joe Blake, who had been acting as his agent and now declined to do so any longer. Agricultural prices were down, the tenants refused to pay their rents, and there was a danger of his being shot. Moore was deeply shocked. He wrote in reply that the refusal of the tenants to pay any rent was

> terrible. What does it mean Communism? If I have never looked into my business at all events I have never committed any follies. I never spent more than five hundred a year and I was told when I came into the properties I had ever so much.[5]

This *cri de coeur* appears in the *Confessions* in attitudinised, exaggerated self-mockery: "That some wretched farmers and miners should refuse to starve, that I may not be deprived of my demitasse at Tortoni's; that I may not be forced to leave this beautiful retreat, my cat and my python – monstrous."

He returned promptly to Ireland and appointed a young, untried but efficient agent, Tom Ruttledge. He was not a ruthless landlord, despite his occasional wild talk; he was not in personal danger in County Mayo in the period of the Land League, and, once he had got his affairs into some kind of order, he then settled down to a very frugal existence indeed in London while he found his feet as a writer.

He denounced the Act of 1881, which reduced rents twenty per cent without reducing interest; this act gave the tenants some rights in the land without, however, destroying those of the landlords. The situation became less tense. Further Land Acts of 1887 and 1891 prepared the way for the Wyndham Act of 1903; the cumulative effect of these acts was the ultimate transformation of Ireland into a land largely farmed by peasant proprietors.

Moore now felt that disaster was inevitable, that the landlords

[5] J. Hone, p. 81.

as a class were doomed and deservedly so. This did not stop him from collecting his rents, nor from despising his fellow landlords as barbarians interested only in horses. His attitude was contradictory, liberal yet deterministic. Eventually he sold his estate to the Land Commission but retained Moore Hall and five hundred acres around it. After repaying various mortgages he received between twenty-five and thirty thousand pounds so that his prophecies of financial ruin were, to say the least, inaccurate. The house was never occupied again after Colonel Maurice Moore, the novelist's brother, who had been living there with his family since 1905 at George Moore's invitation (in the '90s Moore broke the original settlement of the property on this brother, the second son of the family, though they were then on good terms) left it in 1911 as a result of a severe estrangement that had arisen between the brothers. It was burned down by the Republicans during "the Troubles" in 1923 (because of Colonel Moore's loyalty to the Irish Free State, of which he was a Senator) and eventually Moore received £7,000 in compensation. The destruction of the house moved him deeply.

2

Moore spent the winter of 1883-4 in Ireland at Moore Hall, where his mother was living, and in Dublin. He was then finishing *A Mummer's Wife* and gathering material for *A Drama in Muslin*. He knew enough about the contrast in the countryside between cabin and castle, but he needed to study the social glitter and tinsel of the Viceregal court in Dublin and the manœuvres of the receptions, tea parties, and dances.

His subject was, he wrote to J. E. Blanche (urging him to come to an arrangement with his publishers to illustrate the novel – Blanche in fact did design the frontispiece), a "young girls' book". And so he stayed at the Shelbourne Hotel, in Dublin, attended the Levee, the State Ball (which he thought "very grand and imposing") and a Calico Ball given at the Rotunda. He worked on *A Mummer's Wife* in the mornings; afterwards he made the rounds of the drawing rooms and danced; and always he observed. The following winter of 1884-5 he was back in Ireland again, now working hard on *A Drama in Muslin* and waiting eagerly to see how *A Mummer's Wife* would be received when it was published in December. It sold well, and he left Moore Hall for Dublin in January and wrote with some assurance to Colonel Dease, to tell him that he had been in Dublin the previous year in the interests of a book for which he had attended the Levee, the Drawing Rooms, and the Castle Balls. He continued:

> I was not fortunate enough to receive an invitation for a State dinner party. Now, as my book deals with the social and political power of the Castle [*i.e.* Dublin Castle, the centre of administration] in Modern Ireland, I should be glad to attend the Levee in February, if I could make sure of being asked to one of the big dinner parties. My books, as you are probably aware, are extensively read; this particular one will attract a good deal of attention. It would therefore be well to render my picture as complete, as true, as vivid as possible.[6]

Eventually he began to send notes to the Castle by hand and when he was finally told that the lists were closed, he published the correspondence in a nationalist paper, the *Freeman's Journal*, remarking that he was, of course, unable, as he was unwilling, to argue that his social position entitled him to be asked to the Castle, but that he could not refrain from saying that Lord Fingall and Colonel Dease would find it difficult to show he was not. But he had applied for an invitation as a man of letters, for the purpose of studying, not of amusing himself. He had come to the Castle "not as patriot, nor as place hunter, but as the passionless observer, who unbiassed by political creed, comments impartially on the matter submitted to him for analysis".

When *A Drama in Muslin* first appeared in January 1886 in the *Court and Society Review*,[7] it was prefaced by Moore's own account of its actuality. It was a picture of Ireland all complete, Castle, landlords, and land leaguers, and painted by an Irishman. But in this comment he made inaccurate claims for it, and his exaggeration is significant. He claimed that one out of a hundred delicately nurtured daughters of Irish gentry was lucky if she succeeded in marrying a dispensary doctor or a police officer. He based his

---

[6] *Op. cit.*, p. 107.
[7] From 14 Jan. (Vol. II, p. 80) to 1 Jul. 1886 (Vol. III, p. 104).

view of the position of well-educated Irish girls on a hatred of the "marriage market" and the frustration of enforced celibacy which could come from failure to trade efficiently in it. Like Ibsen, he was convinced that woman was more than a domestic animal. In Hone's words, his heroine, Alice Barton, came to Moore first "in vague fragmentary outline as the type of girl who would refuse to acquiesce in the view that to find a husband who would keep her was the first object of life".[8] The theme of the book was, as its final page reminds us, a study of "unmarried girls – the poor muslin martyrs". Moore regarded his heroine as a puritan "but not a sexless puritan". He remarked that if women cannot win their freedom without leaving their sex behind "they had better remain slaves, for a slave with his sex is better than a eunuch".

He had departed somewhat from the role of the detached observer, or rather departed from his own belief that woman was best as an adjunct to man rather than as an independent "advanced" woman. Indeed he had come near to battling for women's rights in this novel. Here he was influenced by Ibsen and later thought it strange that the critics of the 'eighties failed to notice that the theme of *A Drama in Muslin* is the same as that of the *Doll's House*.[9] But he was prejudiced against Ibsen, he wrote, because they were writing on the same subject from a different point of view. His admiration of and sympathy for his heroine (somewhat similar to his subsequent, equally unsentimental, but discerning portrayal of Esther Waters's integrity and bravery) led him to make her, while a puritan, no prig. Alice Barton, for instance, secretly supports May Gould, a harum-scarum sensuous contemporary, while May has an illegitimate child; she begins to write professionally; and eventually, despite her mother's opposition, she marries a dispensary doctor. Thus she apparently fails in the eyes of her own social world but actually finds fulfilment and good fortune in a marriage based on love, respect, and a serious-minded desire on the part of both partners to be useful. The doctor tells Alice when he proposes to her that he does not think they will have more than three hundred a year to live on. She tells him she hopes to make two hundred a year by her writing:

[8] J. Hone, p. 118.
[9] Preface to *Muslin*, London (Heinemann) 1915 (revised version of *A Drama in Muslin*), pp. vii-ix.

"Then we shall bear life's burden equally?"

"No, not quite equally, but as nearly as Nature will allow us."[10]

Moore was, of course, drawing the exception in Alice Barton, but in doing so he was departing somewhat from his earlier Zola-like attitude to his subject. The style of the novel, too, departs from the plainness of his earlier work. He matches some of his subjects with a prose which is resplendent and voluptuous. There is the famous description of the dressmaker's shop in Dublin where Alice and her more beautiful sister, Olive, are equipped for the Castle Ball:

> Lengths of white silk clear as the notes of violins playing in a minor key; white poplin falling into folds statuesque as the bass of a fugue by Bach; yards of ruby velvet, rich as an air from Verdi played on the piano; tender green velvet, pastoral as hautboys heard beneath trees in a fair Arcadian vale; blue turquoise faille Française fanciful as the tinkling of a guitar twanged by a Watteau shepherd; gold brocade, sumptuous as organ tones swelling through the jewelled twilight of a nave; scarves and trains of midnight-blue profound as the harmonic snoring of a bassoon; golden daffodils violent as the sound of a cornet; bouquets of pink roses and daisies, charmful and pure as the notes of a flute; white faille, soft draperies of tulle, garlands of white lilac, sprays of white heather, delicate and resonant as the treble voices of children singing carols in dewy English woods; berthas, flounces, plumes, stomachers, lappets, veils, frivolous as the strains of a German waltz played on Liddell's band.[11]

---

[10] *A Drama in Muslin*, London (Vizetelly edition), 1886, p. 311.

[11] *Op. cit.*, p. 162. J. Hone, p. 120, quotes from Madame Duclaux's article "Souvenirs sur George Moore", *Revue de Paris*, XII (March 1933) for the following anecdote:

> An orchestra of feminine dress which amused the Miss Robinsons (whom Moore used to visit at this period) and to which they added, in the margin of their copy, some final touches of their own: "Everything was represented there, from the light clarinette of the embroidered lace hand-kerchief to the profound trombone of the red flannel pantaloons." "Oh how could you write such a thing Mr Moore"! the sisters exclaimed, as they read the passage out to Moore on his next visit to

There were new literary influences at work on Moore. Milton Chaikin has suggested[12] that Balzac served as a model – in the long soliloquies, in the attitudes displayed towards celibacy and women, and in depictions of various traits of character. Zola and Balzac inspired Moore's choice of theme, and, Chaikin suggests, Balzac's general picture of small town life was particularly influential. He regards Alice Barton as owing something to Mlle Cormon in *Une Vieille Fille* (1836). Flaubert's narrative technique may have been drawn upon, as Graham Owens has suggested,[13] for the contrast between the personal tragedies of the girls and the general tragedy of Ireland. Sir Maurice Bowra has pointed out[14] that the realist and the story-teller in Moore were often contradictory. He was experimenting at this stage to avoid a flat style and was drawing on his reading in various ways: adjectival effects may be based on the practice of the Goncourts, the choice of theme may owe something to *Renée Mauperin*, and Huysmans also may have influenced the suggestive imagery and the symbolism.[15]

Despite all these varied influences Moore managed to create his own kind of exuberance, particularly in describing the social scenes of the Dublin season, the bustle and crowding, the hectic excitement and ensuing enervation. Here is his description of the Castle Drawing Room:

> The slender figures ascending to tiny naked shoulders, presented a piquant contrast with the huge, black Assyrian bulllike policemen, who guarded the passage, and reduced, by

Earlsfort Terrace. "He fell into the trap," Madame Duclaux records, "and defended the phrase which he had never used. We enlightened him . . . but he bore no malice, and was enchanted that we should interest ourselves in his literature, his great and sole preoccupation."

[12] See his article "Balzac, Zola and George Moore's *A Drama in Muslin*", *Revue de Littérature Comparée*, XXIX (1955), pp. 540-2.

[13] Unpublished thesis: *A Study of George Moore's Revisions of his Novels and Short Stories* (University of Leeds), p. 187.

[14] "George Moore", *New Oxford Outlook*, I, 1 (May 1933), p. 46.

[15] See A. J. Farmer, *Le mouvement ésthétique et décadent en Angleterre, 1872-1900*, Paris (1931), *Bibliothèque de la Revue de Littérature Comparée*, tom. 75, p. 90; S. M. Steward, "J. K. Huysmans and George Moore", *Romanic Review*, 25, 3 (Jul.-Sep. 1934); and G-P. Collet, "George Moore et la France: a propos d'un centenaire", *Revue de Littérature comparée*, Vol. 26 (Oct. 1952), pp. 477-9.

contrast, to almost doll-like proportions the white creatures who went up the great stairway. Overhead an artificial plant, some twenty feet wide, spread a decorative greenness; the walls were lined with rifles; and at regular intervals, in lieu of pictures, were set stars made out of swords. There were also three suits of plate armour; and the grinning of the helmets of old time contrasted with the bearskin shrouded faces of the red guardsmen. And through all this military display the white ware tripped to the great muslin market. The air was agleam with diamonds, pearls, skin, and tulle veils. Powdered and purple-coated footmen stood, splendid in the splendour of pink calves and salmon-coloured breeches, on every landing; and as the white mass of silk pushed along the white-painted corridor, the sense of ceremony that had till then oppressed it, evaporated in the fumes of the blazing gas.

But the battle for existence did not really begin until the blue drawing-room was reached. There heat and fatigue soon put an end to all coquetting between the sexes. The beautiful silks were hidden by the crowd; only the shoulders remained, and, to appease their terrible ennui, the men gazed down the backs of the women's dresses stupidly. Shoulders were there, of all tints and shapes. Indeed, it was like a vast rosary, alive with white, pink, and cream-coloured flowers: of Maréchal Niels, Souvenir de Malmaisons, Mademoiselle Eugène Verdiers, Aimée Vibert Scandens. Sweetly turned, adolescent shoulders, blush white, smooth and even as the petals of a Marquise Mortemarle; the strong, commonly turned shoulders, abundant and free as the fresh rosy pink of the Anna Alinuff; the drooping white shoulders, full of falling contours as a pale Madame Lacharme; the chlorotic shoulders, deadly white, of the almost greenish shade that is found in a Princess Clementine; the pert, the dainty little shoulders, filled with warm pink shadows, pretty and com-pact as Countess Cecile de Chabrillant; the large heavy shoulders full of vulgar madder tints, coarse, strawberry colour, enormous as a Paul Neron; clustering white shoulders, grouped like the blossoms of an Aimée Vibert Scandens, and, just in front of me, under my eyes, the flowery, the voluptuous, the statuesque shoulders of a tall blonde woman of thirty, whose flesh is full of the exquisite peach-like tones of a Mademoiselle Eugène Verdier, blooming in all its pride of summer loveliness.[16]

These passages gain in meaning when they are contrasted with the earlier Spinsters' Ball at Ballinasloe:

... lapsing into silence, the girls scanned the ranks for possible partners. Poor Sir Richard, already very drunk, his necktie twisted under his right-ear, was vainly attempting to say something to those whom he knew, or fancied he knew. Sir Charles, forgetful of the family at home, was flirting with a young girl whose mother was probably formulating the details of a new emigration scheme. Dirty Mr. Ryan, his hands thrust deep into the pockets of his baggy trousers, whispered words of counsel to Mr. Lynch: a rumour had gone abroad that Captain Hibbert was going to hunt that season in Galway, and would want a couple of horses. Mr. Adair was making grotesque attempts to talk to a lady of dancing. On every side voices were heard speaking of the distances they had achieved: some had driven twenty, some thirty miles.[17]

This country entertainment warms up:

The harper twanged still more violently at his strings, the fiddler rasped out the agonising tune more screechingly than ever; and as the delirium of the dance fevered this horde of well-bred people the desire to exercise their animal force grew irresistible, and they charged, intent on each other's overthrow. In the onset, the vast shoulders and the *deux temps* were especially successful. One couple had gone down splendidly before him, another had fallen over the prostrate ones; and in a moment, in positions more or less recumbent, eight people were on the floor. Fears were expressed for the tight dresses, and Violet had shown more of her thin ankles than was desirable; but the climax was not reached until a young man, whose unsteady legs forbade him this part of the fun, established himself in a safe corner, and commenced to

[16] *A Drama in Muslin*, pp. 172-3.   [17] *Op. cit.*, p. 88.

push the people over as they passed him. This was the signal for the flight of the chaperons.[18]

And the evening ends with the gentlemen dancing with the maids and finally carousing in the style of one of those parties described so ably in Sir Jonah Barrington's *Recollections*.

Equally well done are the long country evenings, the boredoms of adult conversations for the young girls: May Gould, for instance, finds discussion of the political situations tedious and blurts out her comments tactlessly: "I can't sit here all day listening to you lamenting over the Land League; and, after a certain number of hours, conjecturing whether Mickey Moran[19] will or will not pay his rent becomes monotonous."[20]

Another aspect of Moore's increasing skill is his ability to distinguish between his heroines, the well-born (and some not quite so) girls who have grown up in Galway, been educated at a convent school, and subsequently are presented and dine and dance during the Dublin season. This distinction is achieved partially by description, partially through the idiosyncrasies of their speech. Cecilia, for instance, who is crippled, attacks sensuous life from a religious point of view: the prose she writes is suitably tortuous[21]; her conversations with Alice verge on the hysterical and become bitter and ugly as she realises that Alice is attracted by Mr Harding, the writer with whom she has struck up a friendship in Dublin.[22] Moore explains how "Cecilia's dark and illogical mind can be accounted for." He is also preparing us for her subsequent decision to become a nun:

Her hatred of all that concerned sexual passion was consequent on her father's age and her mother's loathing for him

[18] *Op. cit.*, p. 92.

[19] "Mickey Moran" is the name used by Moore for a typical Irish peasant in *Parnell and his Island*: "His face is expressive of meanness, sullenness, stupidity . . . he reminds me of some low earth-animal whose nature has not yet risen from the soil . . . Mickey is not a Celt but a Fin. Ages ago the Fins were defeated by the Celts and driven into the outlying districts of Connaught; there they should have died; but owing to their extraordinary power of reproduction they are now making headway against superior races."

[20] *A Drama in Muslin*, p. 83.

[21] J. Hone, p. 121, suggests that her style echoed the manner of the Euphuists.   [22] See especially *A Drama in Muslin*, p. 232, *seq.*

during conception and pregnancy; and then, if it be considered that this transmitted hatred was planted and left to germinate in a mis-shapen body, it will be understood how a weird love of the spiritual, of the mystical, was the almost inevitable psychical characteristic that a human being born under such circumstances would possess.[23]

Throughout the novel the froth of gossip lies on the black depths of serious conversation. The minor characters are well drawn. Mr Harding, the writer, with his irony and cynicism, his air of seeing through shams must have been modelled not a little on Moore himself: both share an obvious desire to shock the bourgeoisie.[24] The aged and affected Lord Dungory with his French sayings moves through the book with a convincing consistency.[25] The Ladies Cullen pursue their conversion of souls with a neurotic persistency. And the weak but not unattractive Lord Kilcarney, pursued by Mrs Barton so shamelessly for her daughter, Olive, is drawn with sympathy and skill as he avoids the net and marries Violet Scully, whose mother, unlike Mrs Barton, had watched the combat from afar. There are brief but telling vignettes of various landlords, bureaucrats, and officers matched by those of mothers, vulgar, ambitious or kindly, according to their nature. All have their proper individuality and contribute to the wideness of Moore's picture of Irish life. They move against a background of scenery which is evoked with an economic sensitivity.

Above all else the story holds us. Moore is primarily interested in its human relationships. He shows us the difficulty of resisting the relentless scheming energy of Mrs Barton (a development of Oliver Goldsmith's scheming mother in *The Vicar of Wakefield*); he lets the vapidity of Olive emerge through her pathetic sentences as well as through the pathos of her ignominious failure to elope with Captain Hibbert, just as he gives Alice the weight and wisdom of the new arguments for women having some other

[23] *Op. cit.*, p. 187.   [24] *Op. cit.*, p. 197, *seq.*
[25] In his preface to *Muslin* (1915) he explained that he could not omit the French epigrams without much rewriting and "remembering my oath never to attempt the rewriting of an old book again, I fell back on the exclusion of *A Drama in Muslin* [from the canon of his works] as the only way out of the dilemma."

interest than the capture of a husband, as well as the moral courage
to resist Mrs Barton's machinations and snobbery. But though
Moore is deeply interested in the human relationships his story
is effectively told; he has developed a sense of irony and a skill in
montage. In chapter thirteen, for instance, there is a technically
interesting use of scenes dissimilar yet interdependent. He gives
us an alternating account of the arguments taking place in front
of the big house between the peasants and their landlord and his
agent and those occurring inside the house between Captain
Hibbert, a suitor for Olive Barton's hand and Mrs Barton, the
landlord's wife, who is determined that he will be unsuccessful:

> From the drawing-room window Mrs. Barton watched her
> little selfish soul racked with individual doubt. On one side
> she saw her daughter's beautiful white face becoming the
> prize of a penniless officer; on the other she saw the pretty
> furniture, the luxurious idleness, the very silk dress on her
> back being torn from them, and distributed among a crowd
> of Irish-speaking, pig-keeping peasants.[26]

This is part and parcel of the fabric of the novel. There are
many similar movements throughout its length where we realise
that Moore is giving us a story which is not only exploring the
situation of the very different girls with whom he is primarily
concerned but is also illustrating for us the social life of Ireland
of which they could be considered the flower. This he shows in
all its complexity, from the misery and degradation of the
peasantry, through vestiges of that vulgarity (to be captured
supremely later, in *The Red Charlotte (1894)*, by Somerville and
Ross) which shades into gentility, to the centre of that world of privi-
lege and power whose national *raison d'être* had vanished in 1800
with the removal of government from Dublin to Westminster.

Dublin seemed to Moore, at this particular stage in his life, to
be seedy and second-rate. (When at the turn of the century he
came to live in Ely Place, filled with dislike of England during the
Boer War, enraptured with the aims of the Gaelic League, and
ready to aid the Irish literary movement, it was a different matter,
and a different Dublin that he knew). It was dirty and melancholy.[27]
He disliked it for being provincial:

[26] *A Drama in Muslin*, p. 127.   [27] *Op. cit.*, p. 158.

We are in a land of echoes and shadows. Smirking, pretend-
ing, grimacing, the poor shades go by, waving a mock-
English banner over a waxwork show: policemen and bailiffs
in front, landlords and agents behind, time-servers, Castle
hirelings, panderers and worse on the box; nodding the while
their dollish cardboard heads, and distributing to an angry
populace, on either side, much bran and brogue. Shadows,
echoes, and nothing more. See the girls! How their London
fashions sit upon them; how they strive to strut and lisp like
those they saw last year in Hyde Park. See the young men –
the Castle bureaucrats – how they splutter their recollections
of English plays, English scenes, English noblemen. See the
pot-hatted Gigmen of the Kildare Street Club! The green
flags of the League are passing; the cries of a new Ireland
awaken the dormant air; but the Gigmen foam at their windows and spit out mongrel curses on the land that refuses to
call them Irishmen.[28]

His view of Ireland was, in fact, a torn and contradictory one.
He claimed detachment of viewpoint, but while he recognised the
impossibility and injustice of the situation, one seen by Alice
Barton in *A Drama in Muslin* as having something wrong with it,
where a hundred little houses work to keep one big one in sloth
and luxury, he did not like the alternative prospect, of a peasant
society. In his pamphlet *Parnell and His Island* (1887) we see this
tortured vision most clearly, and it should be read as a gloss on
the comments on the peasants in *A Drama in Muslin* as "surly" and
the general picture of them as menacing and degraded. This
picture is built up steadily. The Bartons' carriage passes "surly"
peasants,[29] again, more atmospherically:

Around them the barren country lay submerged in shadows;
the ridge of the uplands melted into the drifting grey of the
sky, and every moment the hearth-fire of a cabin started into
or disappeared from sight. They burned, steadfast and
solitary, in the dim wastes that stretched from hill to hill, or
were seen in clusters between the dark blowing foliage of the
roadside poplars; and as the carriage passed, on a door-way

[28] *Op. cit.*, p. 159.   [29] *Op. cit.*, p. 39.

full of yellow light, the form of a man was often sketched in menacing black.[30]

Next they are described as having "a look of quiet cunning" as they guess the annoyance the Land League Proclamation will cause the gentry.[31] Their appearance of degradation is emphasised in Moore's descriptions of Mass: "the peasants came, coughing and grunting with monotonous animal-like voices"[32] . . . they "prayed coarsely, ignorantly, with the same brutality as they lived".[33] Yet Moore is aware, always, of the causes. He continues, "Further away a circle of dried and yellowing faces bespoke centuries of damp cabins, brutalising toil, occasional starvation."[34]

He realised their hardships, the inequality of their lot.[35] This is the civilisation which produces the "martyrs in muslin": "In Ireland every chicken eaten, every glass of champagne drunk, every silk dress trailed in the street, every rose worn at a ball, comes straight out of the peasant's cabin." The slums and suburbs are also affected: "this plague-spot is apparent today to every eye; it is visible everywhere, even in the heart of the slums as in the suburbs; it was as if a veil had been drawn revealing the boils with which the flesh of Ireland is covered." Moore contrasted wealth and poverty throughout the novel. Though he denied his humanitarianism fiercely there is in this description of the Dublin streets through which the carriages went to the Castle Drawing Room some of the feeling which informed *Esther Waters*:

> Notwithstanding the terrible weather the streets were lined with vagrants, patriots, waifs, idlers of all sorts and kinds. Plenty of girls of sixteen and eighteen come out to see the "finery". Poor little things in battered bonnets and draggled skirts, who would dream upon ten shillings a week; a drunken mother striving to hush a child that dies beneath a dripping

[30] *Op. cit.*, p. 51.   [31] *Op. cit.*, p. 68.   [32] *Op. cit.*, p. 70.
[33] *Op. cit.*, p. 71. Malcolm Brown, *George Moore: a reconsideration*, p. 23 points out that peasant and church were obsessively connected in his mind with an image of sputum.   [34] *A Drama in Muslin*, p. 71.
[35] Cf. *op. cit.*, p. 144, where Moore stresses the peasants' memories of hunger even in a year of plenty; and, for the effect of luxury on the landlords, *op. cit.*, pp. 94-6. See also *Parnell and His Islands* for the inequality of landlords' and peasants' lives.

shawl; a harlot embittered by feelings of commercial resent-
ment; troops of labourers battered and bruised with toil:
you see their hang-dog faces, their thin coats, their shirts
torn and revealing the beast-like hair on their chests; you see
also the Irish-Americans, with their sinister faces, and
broadbrimmed hats, standing scowling beneath the pale
flickering gas-lamps, and, when the block brought the
carriages to a standstill, sometimes no more than a foot of
space separated their occupants from the crowd on the pave-
ment's edge. Never were poverty and wealth brought into
plainer proximity. In the broad glare of the carriage lights
the shape of every feature, even the colour of the eyes, every
glance, every detail of dress, every stain of misery were
revealed to the silken exquisites who, a little frightened,
strove to hide themselves within the scented shadows of their
broughams: and in like manner, the bloom on every aristocratic cheek, the glitter of every diamond, the richness of
every plume were visible to the avid eyes of those who stood
without in the wet and the cold.[36]

Despite this clarity of vision, despite his recognition of his own
part in it – "I am an Irish landlord, I have done this, and I shall
continue to do this, for it is impossible for me as for the rest of
my clan to do otherwise" – he recognised the fact that the system
was worn-out, and no longer possible in the nineteenth century.
This sense of impending doom runs through the story. It was "a
time of darkness and constant alarms". The landlords –

An entire race, a whole caste, saw themselves driven out of
their soft, warm couches of idleness, and forced into the
struggle for life. The prospect appalled them ... What
could they do with their empty brains? What could they do
with their feeble hands?[37]

And the passage continues, seeing America as an avenging spirit,
and their possible plunge into its arms as terrifying as was that of
the famine-stricken peasants of '49. There is a feeling of retribu-
tion abroad, and violence occurs. A guest at the ball at Ballinasloe
learns[38] that his brother has been shot; there are arrests and

[36] *Op. cit.*, p. 171.   [37] *Op. cit.*, p. 95.   [38] *Op. cit.*, p. 89.

murders and intimidation[39] and more murders and evictions,[40] outrages[41] and then the shock of the Phoenix Park murders.[42] There is talk of Coercion Acts, and then the '82 Bill for the prevention of crime, and the Land League vanishes in 1882,[43] "vanished as suddenly as a card up the sleeve of a skilful conjurer". But this does not mean a solution of the situation. The circumstances of inequality remain. When Olive fails to elope and contracts pneumonia she recovers in a dry bedroom with a steady temperature, but the doctor remarks:

> I attended a case of it some three or four miles from here, but the damp of the cabin was so great that it was impossible to combat the disease. The cottage, or rather hovel, was built on the edge of a soft spongy bog, and so wet was it that the woman had to sweep the water every morning from the floor where it collected in great pools. The poverty that these peasants endure is something shocking. I am now going to visit an evicted family, who are living in a partially-roofed shed fenced up by the roadside. There, in the most sheltered corner, the father, down with fever, lies shivering, with nothing to drink but cold water, nothing to eat but a potato. The wife told me that last week it rained so heavily that she had to get up three times in the night to wring the sheets out.[44]

The doctor goes on to describe why the family was evicted. He is dispassionate; the peasant was an idle fellow, but he got into bad hands. The conclusion is that boycotting was and was not ended, that the fire was only smouldering, that it was only a time of respite for both parties. It is significant that the last act of Alice and her husband before they leave Ireland is to pay the rent of some unfortunate victims of an eviction:

> The cabin was a fair specimen of its kind. It was built of rough stone without mortar, and through the chinks all the winds of heaven were free to wander. There was a potato-field at the back, and a mud-heap in front, and through the

[39] *Op. cit.*, pp. 94-5.   [40] *Op. cit.*, p. 104.
[41] *Op. cit.*, p. 225.   [42] *Op. cit.*, p. 240.
[43] *Op. cit.*, pp. 264-9.   [44] *Op. cit.*, p. 292.

slush the shattered door was approached by stepping-stones. From the exterior it is easy to imagine the interior – a dark, fetid hole, smelling of smoke, potato-skins, and damp. And about this miserable tenement there were grouped a dozen policemen armed with rifles, two men in pot-hats and long ulsters, and a dozen or fifteen peasants come to watch the proceedings. An old woman of seventy had been placed for shelter beneath a hawthorn-bush; six young children clung about their shrieking mother; the man, with nothing but a pair of trousers and a ragged shirt to protect him from the terrible rain, stood a picture of speechless despair on the dung-heap, amid a mass of infamous bedding, and a few wooden stools that had been dragged from the house by the landlord's agents.[45]

What Moore hankered for was the feudal element in this world that was vanishing. His mixed attitudes sharpen the perception of *A Drama in Muslin*, and give it the general all-over view of Irish society which makes its contribution to the Irish novel so valuable.

When Moore came to rewrite *A Drama in Muslin* – it was published as *Muslin* (1915) – he omitted many sections which showed the influence of Zola (though the descriptions of the peasantry which seem Zola-inspired were left). Graham Owens suggests that Moore in his revisions omitted half the social background, *e.g.* the disparaging references to the gentry, and that he also toned down his originally crude attacks on Catholicism, perhaps because he thought he had overdone this and been, as a result, less effective than he wanted to be.[46] The revised version benefited from the removal of various excrescences, and some authorial comment was cut out. But *Muslin* lacks the first version's warts-and-all picture of Ireland. When he wrote *A Drama in Muslin* Moore was trying to be a detached observer, even though his indignation and sympathy kept emerging; he was writing of human situations in a context the end of which then seemed near and this factor sharpened his perceptions. In this process he was exploring his own complex attitudes to Ireland, and as a result he wrote, like Maria Edgeworth, or Disraeli in *Sybil*, out of a sharp

[45] *Op. cit.*, pp. 322-3.
[46] He makes a detailed analysis of the alterations, *op. cit.*, pp. 192-212.

sense of the inequalities of a divided country, an awareness of the
injustice meted out by one section and the ignorance indulged in
by the other.

It may have been his sense that he knew this Irish background
and that it was unlikely his English and French readers would do
so that led him into the moralising comments of the first version
of the novel (see pp. 61 and 263) and its informative passages
(see pp. 52-3, 114-15, 140, 150, 266-7, 279). He tended to hector
his readers unduly[47]; his own complexity of attitudes had to be
worked out. Though he was brought up as a Roman Catholic,
Moore was developing in the 'eighties a hatred of his native
country "and a brutal loathing of the religion I was brought up
in"; though a landlord, he was highly critical of the Irish Establishment, not to mention Mr Gladstone; though he disliked
Catholic peasants and Protestant proprietors alike, he had a hope
of escaping into what has been the real love of most Irish writers,
a love of the natural beauty of Ireland. In *Parnell and His Island*
he thought to seek the picturesque independent of Landlords and
Land Leaguers: "Where the facts seem to contradict, I let them
contradict". In *A Drama in Muslin* Alice Barton escaped from
"the gloom of crime and poverty" he described so frankly in
Parnell and His Island to a useful life in England, the England he
was himself shortly to portray in *Esther Waters*, paying it tribute
in his own way – "Pecksniff done seriously, and if the fact does not
seem impossible, with love".

Moore's contradictions are evidenced in the variety of styles
visible in *A Drama in Muslin*. He was still finding himself as a
writer, as well as an Irishman. His contradictions, however,
contained the humanitarianism he so strongly denounced, and a
love of the Ireland he loathed. *A Drama in Muslin* is a good place
to see these contradictions working themselves out in artistic
form; the skill of the story-teller in Moore triumphs over the
subtleties – and sophistries – of the stylist; and so he captures and
holds attention with a novel in which he conveys a picture of
frustration on a national scale, yet suggests, like Swift, that it was
not inevitable.

[47] Graham Owens, *op. cit.*, p. 208, lists several instances of this, *e.g.*
pp. 2, 33, 67, 76, 84, 173, 194, 226, 235, 247, 256, 324.

Milton Chaikin

GEORGE MOORE'S EARLY
FICTION

"I came into the world apparently with a nature like a smooth sheet of wax", wrote George Moore at the beginning of *Confessions of a Young Man* (1888). Receptivity to impressions and malleability were the most important properties of that nature, which was "free from original qualities, defects, tastes, etc.". As a writer of fiction in the first years of his career, he was indeed subject to impressions of various sorts, entirely French to begin with; and so he became a carrier of French values and styles. But in the course of time, as he continued to depend on French literature less and less, his own literary personality evolved. Its evolution was as much a creation. Moore said to his appointed biographer, Charles Morgan: "Your story is of a man who made himself because he imagined himself, and you must discover when his imagination went with his nature and when against it."

The degree to which Moore depended upon his French sources in his first years as a novelist is startling. He sometimes translated recognisable passages from them into his own works. His main method in his first novels was to borrow fragments from various books – characters, details, relationships, descriptions, phrases, action – and stitch them into a pattern of his own. These patterns had a relevance to his own experience and preoccupations to a great extent, to be sure, but the derivative nature of his fiction at this time is immediately perceptible.

As a writer in the French style, Moore played a valuable part in the transformation of English fiction. France was the principal seedbed of change in the arts at the end of the nineteenth century, the art of fiction not being the least among these. What French writers of fiction had to teach novelists and short story writers everywhere was that they should be artists primarily, that is, creators and masters of form. To be a master of form meant to experiment in methods, to open wide the possibilities of the medium, thus to open vast new possibilities in exploring consciousness and seeing the world. In addition, French writers of fiction cultivated and transmitted the idea of "telling the truth". "Telling the truth" had two meanings. To begin with, it meant a closer attention to detail and a sense that facts, accurately observed, are essential in the literary treatment of human life. It meant the idea that environments, as an historian or scientist might study them, need to be studied and described to reveal human beings as they develop in specific places and times and as they are affected by them. But "telling the truth" also meant the exposure of unflattering realities that exist behind the usual curtain of false pieties. Carried further, it meant alienation from *bourgeois* society and established values, leading to cynicism and pessimism. The totally disaffected novelist undertook the frank exposure of the murky corners of experience and of the mind, dwelling on the sordid and the morbid, showing up the meanness and ignobility of men.

The principal French novelists who began modern fiction were Flaubert, the Goncourt brothers, and Zola – all of whom influenced Moore, Zola most importantly. All were diligent fact-gatherers, students of environments, and tellers of bitter truths. All were devoted to the invention and development of narrative methods, shapes of fiction, and expressive styles. Moore was impressed with the stylistic accomplishments of the realists. He wrote in the *Confessions*:

> One thing that cannot be denied to the realists: a constant and intense desire to write well, to write artistically. When I think of what they have done in the matter of the use of words, of the myriad verbal effects they have discovered, of the thousand forms of composition they have created, how they have remodelled and refashioned the language in their untiring striving for intensity of expression, for the very

ozmazome of art, I am lost in ultimate wonder and admiration.[1]

Zola is often supposed to have had no style. Moore himself directed this barb at his whilom master in the *Confessions*, but his utterances are not famous for their consistency, and in other places his statements are more appreciative of Zola's stylistic qualities. The fact that Zola did have a style is affirmed by Moore's imitation of it. One of its ingredients was the patterning of a passage so that character and surroundings alternate, the effect being repetitive and rhythmic and evocative, the writing driving with increasing intensity to a climax. Moore described this procedure in the *Confessions*:

> I had read the "Assommoir", and had been much impressed by its pyramid size, strength, height, decorative grandeur, and also by the immense harmonic development of the idea; and the fugal treatment of the different scenes had seemed to me astonishingly new – the washhouse, for example; the fight motive is indicated, then follows the development of side issues, then comes the fight motive explained: it is broken off short, it flutters through a web of progressive detail, the fight motive is again taken up, and now it is worked out in all its fulness; it is worked up to *crescendo*, another side issue is introduced, and again the theme is given forth. And I marvelled greatly at the lordly, river-like roll of the narrative, sometimes widening out into lakes and shallow mere, but never stagnating in fen or marshlands.[2]

Moore not only marvelled at Zola's "fugal" procedure but imitated it, depending on his model so closely in his early work that verbal correspondences may be heaped up in embarrassing lists. The marks of Zola's literary personality are otherwise ubiquitous in the first novels: crowd scenes (the author passing mockingly from one petty personage to another); scenes of food consumption; sensitivity to odours; obsessive references to women's bared skin; the glow of lamplight on objects and

---

[1] *Confessions of a Young Man*, New York, 1901, p. 172. This is the same version as the Sonnenschein edition of 1888.

[2] *Op. cit.*, p. 67.

persons; buildings silhouetted against the sky; the languors of women; symbolism; and descriptive set pieces.

The word "naturalism" has been used variously and has been abused. It is most properly used when it applies to realist fiction that is materialist, determinist, pessimistic, and documentary. Zola's fiction has these attributes; it must be used as the touchstone for the literary type known as naturalism. The writing of Flaubert and the Goncourt brothers approaches naturalism and falls into this category in different books, but these authors saw themselves primarily as artists, allowing literary values to dominate their work. Zola indulged in theorising which equated art and science. His theories are absurd as aesthetics, of course, but it is not possible to say they had no place in his own writing or in that of his imitators. A naturalistic novelist was held to be an "experimentalist", that is, he placed a given character in a given environment to see what the outcome would be. Something like this may be said to describe the course of events in Zola's *Thérèse Raquin*. But mainly, as a "scientific" novelist, Zola created a system in which heredity and environment in conjunction ruin a related series of characters.

Zola's characters are "temperaments". They have sensations rather than thoughts, are dominated by "nerves and blood", have no free will. Materialism is the groundwork of everything: man is at one with nature, is governed by the same laws. When man is not natural, perversion of instinct occurs. This idea operates most obviously in sexual relations.

Each of Zola's novels surveys a class, an occupation, a department of society. This segment of the world is presented in accumulations of facts. At his worst, Zola was the fact-monger that Moore in the *Confessions* said he was, but he endeavoured to work up the facts in fused structures, with counterpoint, symbolism, and emotional heavings, and in his best work succeeded.

"That man was the beginning of me", Moore said, honestly, when he heard of the death of Zola; and despite the acidulous comments about him in the *Confessions*, and in later pieces, some of the influence remained as permanent residue.

As statements in the *Confessions* and elsewhere attest, and as we know from a study of the fiction, Balzac was also present at the outset. Balzac was "the great moral influence in my life".

"Thinking of him, I could not forget that it is the spirit and not the flesh that is eternal. . . ." The reader today, very soon perceiving Moore's contradictoriness and arbitrariness, is inclined to doubt all his statements, but the words "moral" and "spirit" here are not empty rhetoric; they describe an element in the make-up of Moore which has been noticed, and sometimes has been accounted for as compromise. But Balzac's influence upon Moore is a better explanation for the moral and idealistic qualities that become visible in his fiction from time to time.

These qualities violate the conception we have of Moore, which is largely the consequence of the artist's self-portrait as it emerges in the *Confessions*, a portrait of a pagan and patrician Aesthete, glorying in beauty, form, and flesh and announcing his scorn of humanity. But the *Confessions* is a humorous book, an extravagant book, a miscellaneous book. We should pay attention to Moore when he quotes himself in a colloquy with Zola on it:

> "Don't you see, my dear friend, that that book is not my real opinion about life and things, but rather an attempt to reduce to words the fugitive imaginings of my mind, its intimate workings, its shifting colours? Has it never come to you to think differently about things? To find your mind in a ferment of contradiction?"[3]

Zola, who was offended by the references to him, said no, he did not change his mind so readily; an opinion is like a heavy piece of furniture, not moved easily. The furniture of Moore's mind, it may be said, slid about with great ease.

By 1885, Moore had read Walter Pater, the fourth revelation by his own count in the *Confessions*. It seems to have been Pater, mainly, who weaned him from Zola:

> I had not thought of the simple and unaffected joy at the heart of natural things; the colour of the open air, the many forms of the country, the birds flying, – that one making for the sea; the abandoned boat, the dwarf roses and the wild lavender; nor had I thought of the beauty of the mildness in life, and how by a certain avoidance of the wilfully passionate,

[3] *Impressions and Opinions*, London (Laurie) 1913, p. 72. Not in the 1891 edition published by Nutt.

and the surely ugly, we may secure an aspect of temporal life which is abiding and soul-sufficing.[4]

It was Pater who convinced Moore that repose and evenness were in tune with his genius rather than the dynamism of Zola – or even the force and passion of Balzac – and that it served the cause of Art better to wander in the flowered field than to roll in the mud. Naturalism was putrid; Zola was vulgar; and it came to him that the Artist preferred the refined to the vulgar. It was not that the true Artist in fiction endeavoured to be "wholesome" or that he needed to obscure the physical realities on behalf of a false purity; he assigned to the physical its place in life, but the physical did not obliterate the mental and spiritual and artistic. Zola was impressed by the physical. In the essay on Turgenev in *Impressions and Opinions* (the essay having first been published in 1888), Moore quoted Turgenev on Zola:

> "Still the same vicious method pervades the book – the desire to tell us what she felt rather than what she thought. *Je me demande qu'est-ce que cela peut me faire si elle sue au milieu du dos ou sous les bras?*"[5]

Zola was too much concerned with the externalities of life, Moore wrote here; he never attempted to grapple with mental problems, his evocation of the human soul was slight. There were two schools of fiction, the thought school and the fact school, Turgenev belonging to the former, Zola to the latter.

Beginning with *A Mere Accident*, his fourth novel, published in 1887, Moore joined the thought school, eschewing physiology and externality, concentrating on characters with complex thoughts and feelings, avoiding the heaping up of minutiae, preferring rather selectivity and suggestivity. Turgenev's "subtle and soul-revealing touches" and his "indications" become the criteria of excellence in the narrative art: "Painters speak of indications; some are peculiarly happy in indications, and an object skilfully indicated has a charm that the complete painting cannot have." Moore tried "indications" instead of "complete paintings", and his novels became slender for a while.

---

[4] *Confessions*, p. 162.
[5] *Impressions and Opinions*, London (Nutt) 1891, p. 67.

Pater, Turgenev, and Huysmans (who was like "a dose of opium, a glass of exquisite and powerful liqueur", in whose style were "the yearning charm of arches, a sense of ritual, the passion of the mural, of the window") supplant Zola as guides to Moore for a while, though Balzac's influence is still to be felt, as is that of other French writers. The fact that Pater was an Englishman and that Moore was led to admire English prose for the first time enabled him to wrestle free from French tutelage, but this was a process that took some time to complete.

2

Moore began his career as a novelist with *A Modern Lover* in 1883, not as a naturalist writer, but as an imitator of French fiction generally. The core of the book is Balzacian, but the technique resembles that of the latter-day realists. This novel is about the social and financial success of an artist, Lewis Seymour, who fails as an artist because he has no integrity. He starts out obscure and poverty-stricken and ends prosperous and socially acceptable, as a painter of rich women. Indeed, his progress is effected by the exploitation of women, for Lewis is a mean cad. The exploited women number three. Gwynnie Lloyd, a chapel-going working-class girl, poses *au naturel* for Lewis to save him from the river, and is forgotten by him. Mrs Bentham, rich and older than Lewis, becomes his companion and supports him secretly, but is later abandoned. The beautiful Lady Helen marries him, and is betrayed in turn. This patterning is what Moore may have meant when he wrote in the *Confessions* that artistic fiction must have a "sense of rhythmic progression" and a "rhythmical sequence of events".

Moore wrote *A Modern Lover* because he wanted to write about love, art, and *la vie mondaine*, three major interests. He was interested in these subjects because French novelists were interested in them before him and because he had had some actual experience in the departments, more or less. He could make use of his knowledge of painting, acquired in an aborted career as an art student, and beat the drums for the New Art, that is, the Art of Truth, unpopular and created by men of integrity. He could act the connoisseur of love and women, particularly the woman of thirty. The woman of thirty was a speciality of Balzac. For some reason, Moore became enamoured of this personage. Was it a literary infatuation, or did the relevant chapters in the *Confessions* refer to a real person? There is no answer available. As for the leisured class, Moore belonged to it himself. His feelings were ambiguous about it, but then so were the feelings of Balzac. In *A Modern Lover* Mrs Bentham and Lady Helen, who belong to it, are sympathetic characters, but most of the other Society people in this novel are Zolaesque caricatures.

Balzac and Zola, these were the major sources for the novel, with the Goncourt brothers contributing a little. Balzac supplied characters, theme and many details, Zola the decoration. Some commentators observe that the original of Lewis must have been the Marshall of the *Confessions*, a ladies' man and second-rate artist, whom Moore envied because of his sophistication, success with women, and artistic facility. There may be something of Marshall in Lewis Seymour, but there is a great deal of Lucien de Rubempré, hero of Balzac's *Les Illusions perdues*. In the 1917 edition of the *Confessions*, Moore announced that the original of Lewis was Lucien, and there is every reason to believe that he was being truthful. The parallels between *A Modern Lover* and Balzac's story are legion. Lewis and Lucien are exceedingly handsome and irresistible to the opposite sex. Lucien is a poet, Lewis a painter. Both acquire wealth and status with the help of women and at their expense. Both lose their integrity. Both are somewhat effeminate in appearance, are timid and awkward at the beginning, etc. Lucy Bentham's original is Louise de Bargeton; Lady Helen has some resemblance to Coralie. The counting of money is incessant in both works. Balzac introduced the theme of money into fiction, said Moore in *Impressions and Opinions*, and Moore followed Balzac's lead. Lewis and Lady Helen fall into debt; Lucien and Coralie fall into debt. There is no point in this episode in *A Modern Lover*; it is simply something Moore lifted from his source. There are other elements in *A Modern Lover* which are superfluous, insufficiently integrated in the whole. Moore was devoted to artistic form, but the shaping spirit is absent from many pages.

The hand of the amateur is too often visible – this is the hand of Amico Moorini, who wrote Moore's worst pages, as Moore ruefully confessed later. There is a passage in which a moustache-twirling Mr Bentham blackmails his wife, in a parody of fourth-rate Victorian fiction – Moorini wrote it. Gwynnie comes back at the end of the novel, pockmarked, and Lewis, amazingly, does not recognise her – Moorini thought that one up.

The style of the writing is Moore's own plain style, quite undistinguished and sometimes awkward, until we reach passages, about love particularly, which wing aloft. Following the example of the later French realists, Moore paints literary pictures, like impressionist paintings in quality, luminous with poetry. Whenever the chance avails, he indulges in a bit of sensuous description. In the essay on Balzac, Moore credits him with the introduction of pictorial writing into fiction, but the credit should go to the later realists. At the beginning, Moore imitated the Goncourt brothers and Zola in this technique, mainly Zola. There are two Zolaesque "fugues" in *A Modern Lover*, the carriage ride in which Lewis and Lucy Bentham are rocked into voluptuosity as impressionistic city scenes pass by, and the ball sequence in which Lucy Bentham's desolation contrasts with the crowd scenes. These are not only Zolaesque, they are virtually plagiarised from Zola's *La Curée*.

The conclusion one comes to as a result of these findings is that in his first novel Moore's capacity for invention was not very great. Indeed, his inventive powers were never his strongest qualification for authorship.

Moore's second novel, *A Mummer's Wife*, published in 1885, was the first and last naturalistic novel he wrote and is strictly Zolaesque. It is an "experimental" novel in the "scientific" sense, in which the central character, Kate Ede, who has a lower-middle-class bent for piety and domesticity, is suddenly immersed in the libertine environment of the theatre world, and comes to grief in the course of time, as a "nervous erethism" sets in. She falls victim to drink and jealousy, indulges in Zolaesque tantrums, and helplessly and progressively sinks into degradation and dissolution. Kate's fate is the result of too rapid a change in "milieu" and of the interaction of two different temperaments, Kate's and Dick Lennox's, the nervous and the sanguine.

Kate meets Dick while she is married to Ralph Ede, an asthmatic and unattractive shopkeeper. We gather that Kate is repressed. The arrival of big, fat, indolent Dick Lennox, theatrical manager, effects her release, and the two elope. The first third of *A Mummer's Wife*, in which a wife, burdened with an offensive husband, commits adultery with a man who is more sexually interesting, is taken from Zola's *Thérèse Raquin*. The correspondence is unmistakable: the doltish husband, the frustrated and latently nervous wife, the third party who is more sexually pleasing, the background of the shop, the presence of an interfering mother-in-law, the adultery – these appear in both novels. The idea of the fatal interaction of nervous and sanguine temperaments also comes from *Thérèse Raquin*.

But Moore was not dependent on a single source: his habit was to take a bit here and a piece there. The alcoholism and psychological disintegration derive from Zola's *L'Assommoir*; the description of Kate's success as a singer owes something to Zola's *Nana*; Kate's languorous reveries are like those of Hélène in Zola's *Une Page d'Amour*, from which Ralph's asthmatic paroxysms late at night were also borrowed. Besides, echoes of Zola of a various kind abound. Spires and roofs are defined against orange-coloured skies, and the firelight plays on the hands. Offensive odours are present on every other page. References are made to the unclad state of women. Characters at the dining table ingest food voraciously. Minor characters in a crowd behave fatuously, as the author's eye passes from one to another.

The instinctual and the subcerebral are prominent elements in *A Mummer's Wife*: languorous reverie wells up in Kate, her fingers itch for needle and thread, a longing for gin assails her "with fury", she scratches Dick's face as her brain "boils with excitement". Kate's psychical failure affords the author a chance to indulge in clinical accounts of physiological decay. Sickbed and deathbed scenes are frequent; on her last bed in the final pages, Kate lies, with distended stomach, withered arms, and wispy hair.

This is very much a book written according to a formula; the formula governs the design of the whole. But this design is partially obscured by pages of details relating to Kate's psychology, the backgrounds of the action, a flock of minor characters. Moore filled pages with theatre information. What is it like backstage, for example? Moore has been backstage with a notebook and will transcribe his notes with thin fictional disguise. How do mummers behave away from the theatre? Moore has been with the second company of *Les Cloches de Corneville*, and tells all. The general effect is tedium. Zola's energy galvanised his own technique, but this energy is lacking in Moore's novel, except in the violent last section.

Moore dwelt too long on all his scenes for real effectiveness, but the quality of the book is further reduced by flat writing. One can be no harsher than Moore himself, years later: "The book isn't written at all; you can't call a collection of sentences, or half-sentences, prose, any more than you can call the inhabitants of a hospital an effective regiment." John Freeman, in agreement, called this kind of writing "merely print". Moreover, the hand of Amico Moorini is seen throughout, in questionable figures of speech, authorial intrusions, and impossible psychology: ". . . the sound of her complaining voice harassed the darkness of the room"; "the suspicion that had for months been gnawing at her heart, serpent-like, opened its jaws to suck her down at once into its monstrous gullet."

Nevertheless, as the first naturalistic novel in English fiction, *A Mummer's Wife* has a certain place in the history of English literature.

Moore's third novel, *A Drama in Muslin*, published in 1886, represents a considerable departure from the naturalism of *A Mummer's Wife*. The central character, Alice Barton, is not a "temperament" like Kate Ede, but has a mind and a will of her own, is admirable in judgment and action, and wins over adversity in the end. Alice, having finished school, finds that the people about her in her home county are fatuous and that country life is empty. Furthermore, the possibility of spinsterhood hangs over all young girls like a cloud. Those who are still eligible conduct a rather remarkable warfare for the few men of standing. Alice recoils in disgust from the degrading marriage scramble, but being rather plain-looking she experiences anguish at the thought that her own love-hunger may remain unsatisfied. In time, she revolts against her sterile environment, particularly against her predatory mother, who would have suppressed her, and succeeds in getting married. Her marriage is not romantic in the conventional sense, but it is fulfilling in a very middle-class way, while ironically some of the other, more obviously attractive maidens in the story may become "muslin martyrs".

This drama of nubility is played out against a background of class warfare in Ireland, involving rent strikes and assassinations, abject poverty, and the frivolity of a threatened landlord class. Ironic contrast is a constant feature of the book. Moore alternates the foreground and background, the silken foolishness of the parasitical upper-class women and the black misery of their surroundings, sometimes in Zola's "fugal" style. One may observe that while Moore does not sentimentalise the peasantry, he is aware of their exploitation, though his sympathies are qualified by a sense of disaster and doom for his own class.

In *A Drama in Muslin*, Moore incorporated much that was garnered from his experience in Ireland and by research there, but the vision and organising principles remain French. Specific borrowings are hard to find, and this indicates that Moore was beginning to exercise greater freedom than before. But one can detect definite traces of Balzac and Zola. Alice, in her great desire to be wed, has a parallel in Mlle Cormon, the old maid of *Une Vieille Fille* – a source supported by verbal echoes. Verbal echoes also indicate that Moore took the theme of the pursuit of husbands by mothers of marriageable young daughters from Zola's *Pot-Bouille*. Balzac was persuaded that provincial life is characterised by triviality and gossip, avarice, rivalry, and widespread celibacy. These elements account for a great deal that happens in *A Drama in Muslin*. The sympathy expressed in this book for the fulfilment of love's desires in marriage is consistent with Balzac's attitudes. But the prose poems that fill the volume are Zolaesque. Some of these, involving synaesthesia and symbolism, are carried to amusing excess: for example, the catalogue of women according to taste ("the sugary sweetness of blondes, salt-flavours of brunettes", "and this allegro movement of odours was interrupted by the garlicky andante . . . that the perspiring arms of a fat chaperon slowly exhaled"). When Moore shook off Zolaism, these extravagances were the first to be sacrificed.

Another element in the novel worthy of mention is the world-hating and man-hating perversity of the Lesbian Cecilia, who turns to mysticism as a refuge. Her pathological condition is a foil to Alice's mental and spiritual health. We have here for the first time the polarisation of life attitudes Moore found in Zola. The idea that religion is life-denying and inhibiting, and a refuge for those who are too sick in heart and mind to love, was a favourite with Moore, and appeared again later in various forms.

A Drama in Muslin is one of Moore's long novels: it is too long and suffers from excrescent passages of "fine writing". But it should be counted as one of the better efforts of his early period. The fundamental conception has value; the description of Irish wretchedness and strife has a certain force; and the character of Alice Barton engages the interest.

A Mere Accident, published in 1887, marks a further deviation from Zolaism in that the art of omission has been conspicuously practised and the "documentation" consists of learned disquisitions reminiscent of Huysmans and Pater. The central character, John Norton, is an intellectual and aesthete, possessing over-refined sensibilities and supersubtle preferences. These are described by the author with some ambiguity: Moore enjoyed the air of learning and rarity which he thought he was creating and at the same time implied that Norton's opinions were signs of morbidity. Norton is said to be afraid of death and afraid of life, recoils from "unspeakable feminality", dislikes upholstery and soft beds, and is enraptured by the sensuousness of Christian ritual.

The ideational basis of the novel is simply the opposition between nature and health on one side and religiosity and neuroticism on the other; in this it resembles the polarity of Alice Barton and Cecilia, and clearly derives from Zola. John Norton, flirting with religion and averse to sex, falls in love with Kitty, and the ensuing struggle within him is resolved by "a mere accident": Kitty is ravished by a tramp whom she encounters accidentally and later, in acute disturbance, falls to her death. In Zola's *La Faute de l'abbé Mouret*, the ascetic priest Serge Mouret falls ill with a nervous disorder, is introduced into the garden of Paradou, where he meets Albine, and is cured in his transgression with her. Serge feels guilt, experiences inner conflict, and in the end overcomes his natural self, whereupon Albine asphyxiates herself with the perfume of flowers. There is no doubt about the connexion. The leitmotifs of *La Faute* are reproduced in *A Mere Accident* – the colour of white, the stain of the world on that whiteness, the overabundance of flowers.

It is commonly held that Moore's cousin Edward Martyn

served as life model for the portrait of Norton. Martyn found life vulgar, was abstinent, and had an aversion for women; his room was monastic and he collected French Impressionists. All this is true of John Norton, but Moore combined literary and life sources in the composition of this work, as he did in other works.

The piecing together of patches, which continued to be Moore's method of composition, embraced Pater and Huysmans as well as Zola. Norton's taste for obscure Latin authors – Lactantius, Prudentius, Sedulius, St Fortunatus – derives from Huysmans, and one passage describing Kitty's horror is a revision of a nightmare in *A Rebours*. Norton's interest in Hellenism is Paterian, and a deliberate chastening of the emotionalism hitherto cultivated is evident in the word-paintings and set pieces. Some passages are designed to produce effects of quiet grace:

> How fair a prospect of southern England! Land of exquisite homeliness and order; land of town that is country, of country that is town; land of a hundred classes all deftly interwoven and all waxing to one class – England. Land encrowned with the gifts of peaceful days – days that live in thy face and the faces of thy children.[6]

Elements of Balzac and Zola could be linked in the first novels without serious disharmony, but greater difficulty arises when Huysmans's misanthropy, Pater's aloofness and idealisation, and Zola's championship of sexual fulfilment are grafted together. Moore's effort to write a more intellectual book and one less solidly grounded in "externality", a book depending on "indications" rather than filled-in spaces, left him exposed as a novelist. The patchwork nature of the composition is too obvious. The ending violates the rule of logical conclusion. The desire to be impressive is very evident. And very little in the book is credible.

A Mere Accident began a period of experimentation which produced four novels. Of these he saw fit to preserve only one, *Spring Days*.

Spring Days, published in 1888, is surprising because the style is natural and unforced – only traces of French mannerisms remaining – and instead of the usual seriousness we find here a

[6] *A Mere Accident*, London (Vizetelly) 1887, p. 5.

lightness of spirit and a comic turn. The frequent laughter of characters, for example, despite their complaints and worries, contributes to this book's freedom from care. Many fragments capture the unforced absurdity of daily experience:

> "What did she say to that?"
> "She was just going out to walk with her pugs. Angel began to – you know, and for the moment she could think of nothing else; and when the little beast had finished I had forgotten the thread of my argument."[7]

Presumably the characters and action were drawn mainly from life, the novel reflecting Moore's good feeling about his Saxon friends at Southwick at the time of composition, and about their upper-middle-class life in the countryside. No one in the book has much claim to intelligence, all the characters are rather ridiculous, but their foibles are regarded with tolerant amusement; the acid of French realism is absent. The story is mainly about Frank Escott, who is excessively sentimental, it seems, and will succeed in nothing but getting married. First he becomes engaged, rather pointlessly, to one of the Brookes girls, but this engagement is broken. Then he is enamoured of a barmaid, and at the end of the book we suspect he is bound for the marriage altar, sacrificing his inheritance. But nothing matters very much, really, the comment on life is slight, the relevance to anything important is minimal, and the reader will soon forget what he has read. Some critics have been very hard on this book: "tepid" and "arid" are words used to describe its quality. But Moore himself said, after rereading it years later, that there was a zest in it. According to him, Edward Martyn and other discriminating readers liked it. Martyn's comment was "It is the most original, it is like no other novel, and that is why people didn't understand it." It *is* like some novels that have been written since, somewhat satirical, somewhat ludicrous, about small people and small doings. Moore should at least get high marks for unpretentiousness and for the fact that his characters, unidimensional as most are, have some life and are not the carbon copies of other characters in French novels.

[7] *Spring Days*, London (Vizetelly) 1888, p. 20.

A Mere Accident, Spring Days, and *Mike Fletcher,* the last published in 1889, form a sort of trilogy, all three concentrating on men, each central character having a different psychological nature, and each failing to meet the challenge of existence. John Norton and Frank Escott have featured roles in *Mike Fletcher,* the first continuing his masochistic and world-denying mysticality to the extent of burning his poems, the second finally marrying his low-born mistress, losing his inheritance, and allowing himself to sink into an impecunious but happy domesticity. Other characters of Moore's past creation also make their appearance: Lewis Seymour, now grown fat, puts in a fleeting appearance; his wife, Lady Helen, has a bigger role, for she commits suicide in these pages; and the ubiquitous Harding, spokesman for Moore, who threads his way through many of his books, uttering little paragraphs of the new criticism, also holds forth here.

The world of *Mike Fletcher* is the world of bachelordom, filled with gay parties, love, (supposedly) clever talk, and talent. Typical scenes of restaurants, music hall, and the Temple pass before our eyes. Dissipation is the rule of life. The author, in writing about all this, seeks sophistication. He tries for intensity of language, for the ozmazome. Little prose poems are everywhere. And indeed it must be acknowledged that in the department of "fine writing" his skill has become impressive – his style is now a far cry from the wooden prose of the first novels, and obvious dependence on French models is slight. Published the year before, the *Confessions* had achieved the stylistic excellence of a mature writer. Some of this quality is present in *Mike Fletcher.*

The title character is a modern Don Juan, irresistible to women, effective in everything except that he cannot seduce the pure-hearted Lily. Mike Fletcher is adventurous, courageous, strong, skilful. " 'I can make nothing of it; there was never any one like me. . . . I could do anything, I might have been Napoleon or Caesar.' " He is very good at cheating at cards, too. He thinks and talks about the varieties of love. " 'How delicious love in a country house is!' " His libertinism has unlimited scope, but the worm of discontent gnaws away. Mike goes from one hobby to another, politics, the Orient, vice, but everything turns to ashes. He even thinks that marriage may give him grace; marriage with Lily is a possibility, but she is phthisic and dies on the eve of elopement. And so in the end, full of ennui, Mike shoots himself in the middle of some purple prose.

Moore became convinced of the badness of *Mike Fletcher* quite soon after publication and thereafter did not wish to hear of it again. The trouble was that the immaturity that was part of his nature was in command in the composition of this book. Pretentiousness bobs up everywhere. The face of the absurd Amico Moorini is often visible behind the screen of sophistication and *écriture artiste*.

Vain Fortune, Moore's next novel, published in varying versions in 1891, 1892, and 1895, welds two themes: the failed writer and the hysterical young girl. Both were favourites of the later French realists – Zola's account of a neurotic girl in *Une Page d'Amour* (mentioned in *Mike Fletcher*, incidentally) may be cited as a parallel at least – but Moore was operating with a certain amount of freedom in the vague climate of French fiction. There is a likelihood, also, that Moore's interest in the struggles of a would-be writer living up to the highest ideals of art – his self-doubts, his feelings of satisfaction and his frustration at the writing table – had something to do with his own creative anxieties and recent sense of failure.

Vain Fortune reminds one of Turgenev. It is short; it is composed largely of dialogue; the writing is natural and straightforward, the author having left behind the extravagances of *Mike Fletcher*. A melancholy air is present, particularly at the end.

Hubert Price, the writer, is the hope of those who expect a vigorous new drama, but he is an "intentionist", whose aspirations exceed his reach. In Price's travail to write well, he sinks temporarily to the lower depths and counts shillings and pence. At this point, he inherits a fortune, which should have gone to a young girl of eighteen, Emily Watson. Instead of resenting him, she falls in love with him, but he prefers her older companion, Julia Bentley. Emily falls into an irrational jealousy: she keeps to her bed in the darkness, refuses food, and is unable to sleep. She would be content simply to keep Hubert and Julia apart. When she fails in this, she commits suicide, thus blighting their marriage. At the same time, it becomes clear to Price, somehow, that he will never succeed as an author. But at least Julia is his wife. " 'Hubert!' It was Julia calling him. Pale and overworn, but in

GMMA D

all her woman's beauty, she came, offering herself as compensation for the burden of life."

The characterisation of the hypersensitive young girl of eighteen is effective, but *Vain Fortune* does not really hold together – the two themes do not cohere, despite Moore's effort to draw a parallel:

> In both lives there had been a supreme desire, and both had failed. "Hers was the better part," he said bitterly. "Those whose souls are burdened with desire that may not be gratified had better fling the load aside. They are fools who carry it on to the end. . . ."[8]

In *Esther Waters*, published in 1894, Moore turned away from the "evocation of thought", from the portraits of upper-class, artistic, and bohemian personalities and milieux, to the story of a simple life. It is a story of the life of a servant, dealing with "the common bread of humanity". The choice of subject is an occasion for comment, in view of the announced patrician prejudices of the Aesthete who wrote it and his obvious preference for refined and complex matter. Malcolm Brown has suggested that the change in direction may have been due to discouragement over the four books that preceded *Esther Waters* and to a desire to secure for once a large audience. But these statements of motivation are speculative and somehow do not seem to reflect the true Moore, who did compromise sometimes by watering down the French confrontation with the realities, but who was more independent than these suppositions suggest.

We should credit Moore's account that he was struck by the possibilities of the subject while reading the newspaper. The fact that the French realists had thought servants worthy of literary treatment must have done nothing to dissuade him from the enterprise. In the view of such disaffected writers as Flaubert, only the humblest have any worth in an unworthy society. The contrast of that worth with their elementary natures provided an ironic bite that was particularly satisfying to Flaubert. Certain qualities of *Esther Waters* are Flaubertian, but his acrid pessimism is missing. The central character is invested with warmth and sympathy throughout, and the last part is imbued with the twi-

[8] *Vain Fortune*, London (Henry) 1891, p. 292.

light sadness that characterises the end of *Vain Fortune*. Flaubert was compassionate, but his compassion is well covered by an apparently cold impersonality, as in *Un Coeur simple*, which is also about a servant. There are traces of *Un Coeur simple* and other writing by Flaubert in *Esther Waters*, but only a few. Moore himself was inclined to acknowledge the tutelage of Flaubert in the 'nineties, when the French writer's mastery was hailed on all sides: "Open *Esther Waters* and read that last scene where she meets her son after a long separation. What an embrace! That, my dear friend, is pure Flaubert."

Most of what is instinctual in Esther relates to her passionate motherhood: ". . . she existed like an atmosphere about the babe, an impersonal emanation of love. She lay absorbed in this life of her life, this flesh of her flesh, unconscious of herself as a sponge in warm sea-water." However, she is not a creature entirely at the mercy of internal and external circumstances, but a person of spirit, who emerges from her struggle with a harsh environment, bruised yet with some shred of victory and a considerable degree of humanity. Thus the melancholy and resignation of the end are qualified by the satisfaction of her achievement in bringing up her child against odds.

Because he was dealing with the daily life of a servant, with simplicities of behaviour and environmental influences, Moore thought fit to resort to his earlier method of searching examination of character in action during an extended period of time and with the full "documentation" of milieux. As a result, we have in this novel numerous sketches of the two worlds Esther lives in, domestic service and horse-racing. Moore employed, in the main, a plain and unaffected prose style. There are some deficiencies in the fictional art: the passage of time is not always adequately managed and Esther's motherhood is forgotten for too many pages where horses and bets take over. In psychological matters, however, Moore may be credited with an unremitting honesty, an avoidance of the melodramatic, the sentimental, and the cliché. The characterisations are convincing. Solidity is achieved also by a realistic treatment of the surroundings. Of all Moore's books, readers have liked this one best. The warmth of Esther's portrayal and the appeal to their sense of justice have no doubt played a part in their response to it.

But if there is a note of social protest in the novel, it was not intended, despite Moore's later ironical reference to his "good book" and his citation of its beneficial effects. His statement in a later Preface is a fair summation of his attitude in the writing of *Esther Waters*:

> The teaching of "Esther Waters" is as little combative as that of the Beatitudes. Betting may be an evil, but what is evil is always uncertain, whereas, there can be no question that to refrain from judging others, from despising the poor in spirit and those who do not possess the wealth of this world, is certain virtue. That all things that live are to be pitied is the lesson that I learnt from reading "Esther Waters" . . .[9]

Celibates, published in the following year, consists of three short pieces of fiction, which mark a return to economy in style and to temperamental chastity as a subject. Moore's briefer fiction, one notes, was coincident with a widespread interest in the short story in this decade.

The longest of the three, "Mildred Lawson", describes a young woman who is constitutionally frigid but is at the same time an incurable trifler with the affections of men. Selfish and cruel, she makes a succession of men fall in love with her and jilts them. One of them, incredibly, dies of shock. In the end, Mildred remains alone, neurotically and virginally unhappy. A good deal of the foreground and background suggests Balzac: newspapers, politics, society, love, celibacy. The model for Mildred was probably the Duchesse de Langeais, the coquette in Balzac's novel of that name. The Duchesse is not afflicted with frigidity, but as a cold and selfish woman of the aristocracy she plays with the affections of the Marquis de Montriveau. Both Mildred and the Duchesse are adepts in the art of teasing men and shielding themselves from the ardours of their "lovers" with scruples, irritability, and disputatiousness.

The second story, "John Norton", the revision of *A Mere Accident*, is interesting because the rewriting brings to our notice the changes in Moore's style. The tendency is toward reduction

---

[9] *Esther Waters*, Chicago, 1901, pp. viii-ix. This is the same version as the 1899 Walter Scott edition, which was a revised text.

and simplification. The writing is more scenic, and even greater stress is put on dialogue than in the original novel. The author is more detached; whatever fervour is to be found in the original is diminished; the excrescences – scene paintings and intellectual "documents" – have been whittled away. Most of the reminders of Pater, Zola, and Balzac are gone, and Moore's new enthusiasm, Wagner, has been added to the intellectual apparatus. But the revision did not satisfy Moore, and the story was not admitted in any form to the official edition of his works.

Agnes Lahens, in the story of which she is the title character, inclines toward a cloistered life, not because of hereditary disposition, but because she has been brought up in a convent and recoils from the vicious society of her mother's drawing room. The interest of the story lies in the corruption of this social group, which is described according to the Balzacian model. The relations between the sexes are unconventional, the characters are dissolute and wicked. Contrasted with all this is Agnes's father, who lives in the most abject humiliation in an attic room and is very paternal, a mark of Balzacian worth. When Agnes goes back to the convent, we are sympathetic, and her return is to be interpreted as a comment on corrupt worldliness.

3

A review of Moore's early fiction thus reveals a writer who began as a rather slavish imitator and by 1895 acquired substantial freedom as he sought to sift out what truly belonged to himself and to form a style of his own. The variety of approaches and styles testifies to considerable uncertainty and a willingness to change.

Balzac, whose influence was present from the beginning, gave him moral balance, and whenever a strain of idealism is discovered in his fiction, as in *Mike Fletcher* surprisingly, or when marriage is treated with sympathy, or when the good Alice Barton imparts her sense of decency to *A Drama in Muslin*, the shadow of Balzac is to be apprehended. (We may suppose that some of the goodness may be Moore's own, concealed as it was behind the pose of objectivity.) But Balzac was a man with a passion for life, and if love loomed large in Moore's vision Balzac did not discourage him. Also from Balzac, Moore learned to despise the smallness of life in fashionable society. Moreover, it is to be feared that some of Moore's bad literary judgment owes a good deal to the master's melodramatic and sentimental excesses.

It was not difficult to correlate Balzac's influence with Zola's. It was Zola's style that attracted Moore, as well as his astonishing theories about literature, which he applied in *A Mummer's Wife*. But Zola was too common, and his energy was not really harmonious with Moore's inclinations. He therefore gladly adopted Pater as counterpoise after 1885 and opted for a milder view of life. At the same time, he rejected the piling up of externalities in favour of a greater selectivity. He was an Aesthete from the start, really, and was bound to turn away from the everyday to the various forms of the refined and the rare, from obvious styles to one more subtle – a subtle style possibly being a simple one. The refined and the subtle were set aside temporarily in *Esther Waters*, for which Moore resumed the everyday.

Moore's conception of life and the world and art, as it emerges in his work, is quite simple. One great excellence in life is love's fulfilment, and another is the high vocation of the artist. The artist turns to the theme of love again and again, examining its infinite variety, turning love into beauty. He also champions love against its foes. One foe is religious asceticism, which teaches that the instinctual life is evil; another is the corruption of the world, which causes it to sicken. The artist, resisting the temptation of the world and struggling to express his vision, does the noblest work of man. But the life of man is pervaded by sadness, for aspiration exceeds the reach, circumstances conspire against happiness, disappointment is the rule of life. The sound that is heard in his work is "like a wind sighing over bog water".

The literary artist, if he had integrity and wrote at the end of the nineteenth century, sought beauty in style. Moore started off with the enormous impediment of not knowing spelling, punctuation, and grammar, let alone the secrets of graceful prose. Largely for this reason, he performed heroic labours in writing his books. The marvel is that he became a master stylist. In the period under review, his first task was to put behind him the altogether undistinguished manner of the beginning, with all its crudities; the next task was to slough off French manner, mannerisms, and language. He wrote without pretentiousness in *Spring Days*, which has only a few traces of French fiction, and wrote well. *Confessions of a Young Man* was stylistically more ambitious. By 1888, he was capable of writing prose redolent of ninetyish decadence with expertise:

> And should she *not* visit his rooms? If the complex and various accidents of existence should have ruled out her life virtuously; if the many inflections of sentiment have decided against this last consummation, then she will wax to the complete, the unfathomable temptress – the Lilith of old – she will never set him free, and in the end will be found about his heart "one single golden hair". She shall haunt his wife's face and words (should he seek to rid himself of her by marriage), a bitter sweet, a half-welcome enchantment; she shall consume and destroy the strength and spirit of his life, leaving it desolation, a barren landscape, burnt and faintly scented with the sea. Fame and wealth shall slip like sand from him. She may be set aside for the cadence of a rhyme, for the flowing line of a limb, but when the passion of art has raged itself out, she shall return to blight the peace of the worker.[10]

Mike Fletcher, too, was designed to capture this quality, but Moore's fictional imagination here was not equal to the conception, and so the absurdities that lurk behind the gay artifice of the *Confessions* obtrude in the novel. Thereafter, simplicity was cultivated. By 1895, the decorative touches are scarce, and a rare directness is to be encountered.

In composition and in the art of fiction, Moore was, in the first two decades of his career, a very uneven writer. He was perfectly capable of writing with what Charles Morgan calls a "virulent badness". Amico Moorini "was forever popping up, seizing the pen and writing nonsense". Moore submitted to a very taxing, exacting self-education to excise this element from his writing, to transform it. In addition, he had the problem of how to form a unity of all the pieces he wished to put together. This problem did not exist in the composition of the *Confessions*, the arbitrariness of whose contents is a virtue. But a novel presents another case. The arbitrariness of the miscellaneous contents of *A Mere*

[10] *Confessions*, pp. 60-1.

Accident, *Mike Fletcher*, and *Vain Fortune* is distressing. At length Moore's evolving prose style would solve a good deal of the problem by suspending the miscellany in its flow.

In his restless experimentation with form and style, regardless of his originality and success, Moore made a significant contribution to the development of modern fiction, and this may be considered his most valuable achievement between 1883 and 1895. He was instrumental in gaining acceptance among English-language readers for the ideas that the shape of a piece of fiction depends upon "rhythmical sequence" rather than plot, that the occurrences in a novel should be natural and not contrived, that the sensuous is an important element in the apprehension of fictional truth, and that a carefully written language is as essential in fiction as character and action.

William C. Frierson

GEORGE MOORE COMPROMISED
WITH THE VICTORIANS[1]

Not many years ago Ford Madox Ford said that George Moore's aloofness from life had generally kept him from being considered in critical discussions, but that there was not a critic "with any pretensions to knowledge of letters who would not acknowledge when challenged that Moore was infinitely the most skilful man of letters of his day – the most skilful in the whole world". This tribute, coming as it does amid Ford's damaging comments on Moore's cold and clammy personality, serves at least to place Moore as a very important modern. But there are many other reasons why Moore has been omitted from critical discussions, not least among which is the difficulty of placing him satisfactorily. To speak of him with authority one must read a vast quantity of poor and sloppy fiction and disentangle it from what is undeniably first-rate; and one has to be aware of the author's different intent in each of his numerous fresh starts. There is no such thing as a typical George Moore novel. And again, when we compare the heterogeneous mass of Moore's novels with the uniform suave urbanity and originality of his critical and autobiographical writings, we are confronted with a contrast that does not lend itself to ready generalisations. In the nonfiction writings Moore reveals himself as a thoroughly modern spirit, even as far back as the eighteen-eighties. But in his fiction of the 'eighties and 'nineties there is much tameness, timidity, and compromise, and we even see occasional capitulation to the conventional moralising that Moore so bitterly attacked in his critical writings.

[1] [Reprinted from *Trollopian* (now *Nineteenth-Century Fiction*) I, No. 4 (March 1947), pp. 37-44.]

The essentials of Moore the modern are sufficiently revealed to us in the *Confessions*, which was written in the years preceding 1888. The *Confessions* has been called "an attempt to introduce diabolism to the English mind". But it is more than this. It is an attempt to be painfully honest about some things – about egoism, for example. About man's primary desire for satisfaction of the senses and the esteem of his contemporaries. About the satisfaction that money gives. Moore's impersonation knows himself and his desires, and is not ashamed. If, as Floyd Dell says, Moore has the "man-about-town's attitude towards women" and fills "pages with maudlin phrases about marble, perfumes, palm-trees, lingerie and moonlight", he is, after all, not far away from the sophisticate of postwar days. Moore freed himself rigorously from the prejudices of nationality, he had a proper respect for formative influences, he was impervious to transcendental sophistries. I doubt that he would have used the cold-blooded word "sex" even if he had known of its future implications, but he was prophetic of the "separateness" and "otherness" which D. H. Lawrence so acclaims: he evoked the charm of flowers, silks, scents, and sin. He was modern in his "delighted acceptance of actuality". He was modern in his revolt against convention, restraint, and taboo. Moore the modern responded to the scientific materialism of his day, and he welcomed the new art of naturalism based upon science and devoid of plot and conventional idealisations. He was dazzled and converted. How would the England of 1883 respond to a naturalistic novel written by an Englishman?

Moore wrote *A Modern Lover*. The theme is naturalistic enough. A young artist, only moderately talented, rises to fame and fortune through the influence of women. Lewis Seymour is an amoral artist who lives for his art, his emotions, his success. A liaison with a woman of quality takes place. So far so good. Yet the novel is tame and discreet. The carnal elements are limited to handclasps and to two furtive kisses.

Moore's biographer is not here helpful. Did the Moore of moonlight, lingerie, and perfumes give in the original manuscript a visual portrayal of the modern lover in action, and did the publisher tone it down? We cannot say. What we do know is that Moore's novel, tame as it was, met with difficulties. Two ladies living in the country wrote to the director of one of the circulating-library systems, and Moore's novel was removed from library circulation. The circulating libraries usually bought 400 copies of all three-volume novels, to keep what amounted to a monopoly. Moore was virtually blacklisted from publishing any more three-volume novels. No publisher would take the risk. What then?

Moore persuaded Vizetelly & Co., translator and publisher of Zola's novels, to engage in racket-busting by issuing Moore's next novel, *A Mummer's Wife*, in one volume. And Moore thought he had learned a lesson. In his first novel the man who had violated the moral code profited from the venture. This was taboo. Even as late as 1892, W. H. Mallock carefully stated the Victorian restriction: "In the English fiction of today it is a universal rule that the men, and especially the women, with whom the reader is invited to sympathise, shall all stop short of one another at a certain point, whatever may be their dispositions of circumstances. It is also a rule equally universal that any grave transgression of the moral code shall entail on its transgressors some appropriate punishment, or, at all events, that it shall not end in their happiness." So *The Mummer's Wife* not only avoided the intimacies of carnal relationship, but provided for a moral, though naturalistic, end. The story, you will recall, is that of Kate, the wife of an invalid, leaving her responsibilities to become the mistress and later the wife of the director of an opera-bouffe company. Kate, unaccustomed to the fast tempo of the new life, drinks casually with the actors but without the discipline she would have possessed had she been accustomed to drinking. She sinks to prostitution and is an ill-tempered hussy at her death.

The book, thus making its bow to Nemesis, met with some success. When it had gone into its fourth edition in 1885, Moore launched a pamphlet entitled *Literature at Nurse, or Circulating Morals*, an attack upon the circulating-libraries. Moore not only had his private grudge against Mr Mudie, director of one of the chains, but Mr Mudie had declared himself as being against all naturalistic novels, and Moore at this time was still the champion of naturalism. The pamphlet reads, in part:

Instead of being allowed to fight, with and amid, the thoughts

and aspirations of men, literature is now rocked to an ig-
noble rest in the motherly arms of the librarian. That of
which he approves is fed with gold; that from which he
turns the breast dies like a vagrant's child; while in and out of
his voluminous skirts run a motley and monstrous progeny,
a callow, a whining, a puking brood of bastard bantlings, a
race of Aztecs that disgrace the intelligence of the English
nation. Into this nursery none can enter except in baby
clothes; and the task of discriminating between a divided
skirt and a pair of trousers is performed by the librarian. . . .
It is certain that never in any age or country have writers
been asked to write under such restricted conditions; if the
same test by which modern writers are judged were applied
to their forefathers, three-fourths of the contents of our
libraries would have to be condemned as immoral publica-
tions. . . . To analyze you must have a subject; a religious or
sensual passion is as necessary to the realistic novelist as a
disease to the physician. . . . Let us renounce the effort to
reconcile these two irreconcilable things – art and young
girls. . . . And that the nineteenth century should possess a
literature characteristic of its nervous, passionate life, I hold
is as desirable, and would be as far-reaching in its effects, as
the biggest franchise bill ever framed.[2]

In so protesting, George Moore wrote what might be termed
the *Areopagitica* of modern fiction. But we may also call the
pamphlet his swan song as a realistic artist. He had followed a
theory, an exacting theory, to the limits of public acceptance, and
had loudly declaimed his objections to restraint. But England still
preferred the realism of Jane Austen, and Moore wanted to be
popular. Well, then, he would write like Jane Austen. He would
amuse himself with the social life of Dublin and portray the
marriage market and the husband hunt. And to force the circulating-libraries of Messrs Smith and Mudie to take his books, he
arranged for serial publication in a newspaper and accepted the
additional censorship that serial publication demands.

The ban of the circulating-libraries was not the only ban that
Moore was fighting. Smith and Mudie owned a large number of

---

[2] *Literature at Nurse, or Circulating Morals*, London (Vizetelly) 1885.

bookstores. These bookstores sold newspapers. They could not ban a newspaper. And since they could not ban a newspaper, they could not logically ban a novel published in a newspaper.

According to Moore, the effort was unsuccessful. And he asked Mr Faux (pronounced Fox), representing Smith, why he would ban a novel like *A Drama in Muslin* from circulating-library use. Mr Faux, who was slyly hypocritical, remarked that one of the feminine characters, Alice Barton, did not "believe in the divinity of our Lord and would not go to church". And then, too, an unmarried Christian had a baby. This would never do! Mr Faux suggested as a model for Moore – Anthony Trollope!

In *A Drama in Muslin*, as we know, there is much lively and casual social chatter. And with naturalistic concern Moore follows the fortunes of four different types of young womanhood. To satisfy further his artistic conscience, he follows Huysmans in graphic delineations of atmosphere. Yet with this novel a retrogression has begun. But he was still avowedly a partisan of Zola. "To me", he said, "Emile Zola is a great epic poet and he may not be inappropriately termed the Homer of modern life."

I doubt that Moore realised the violence he was doing to his own nature. He was trying to be popular and to write naturalistic novels and to imitate Jane Austen all at the same time. The result is that as a novelist he disintegrated during the years when he should have been reaching the height of his powers. A decline set in that lasted nineteen years. He occasionally did splendid work – as in the last quarter of *Mike Fletcher* and in the long short story, "Mildred Lawson". But generally there is frustration and uncertainty and evasion – all of which is unhappily capped by occasional moralisings and a decision to write sympathetically of religious preoccupations. He returned to writing first-rate novels only in *The Lake*, 1905, and *The Brook Kerith*, 1916, when he became again a critic of religious beliefs.

To illustrate my point I must return to the novels of the interim. *A Drama in Muslin* was followed the next year by *A Mere Accident* – a sympathetic study of a young man of monastic ideals, John Norton, who came under the influence of the Jesuits. Norton is fond of a girl, but a new turn is given to the story when a tramp rapes her and when she later commits suicide. Critics universally attacked the ending, and George Moore weakly admitted sometime later that the story was an experiment. The next year, there appeared *Spring Days*, which was a calamity.

This novel shows Moore returning to serial publication in a newspaper. The novel begins with a bellicose preface reminiscent of Poe in one of his defensive and vain moods. The author attacks "an artificial, vicious, and decadent society" which is represented by "a restricted and conventional literature". But his own novel is artificial, restricted, and conventional. Moore salved his artistic conscience only by avoiding a happy ending. Yet he descended to the lowest depths of moralising. After Frank, ineffectual artist and heir to Mount Rorke, has given up a distiller's daughter because of a purely sentimental love for a barmaid, Moore moralises in words proper only to a *bourgeois* and sentimental Tory:

> A man's struggle in the meshes of a vile love are as pitiful as those of a fly in the meshes of a spider. . . . A man's love of a common woman is as a fire to his vitals. . . . It is a cancerous disease, but it cannot be cut out as a cancer. . . . All good things, wealth and honour, are forfeited to it.[3]

There is a full page of this, and I have read it many times to be sure that Moore is not being merely ironical. But no. Moore has just about capitulated to what he interprets as the public's desire for fiction. Strangely enough, the *Confessions* came out the very same year. In the *Confessions*, we recall, Moore has turned away from naturalism and toward Huysmans. But nothing in Huysmans could have inspired *Spring Days*. The author was potboiling.

He was not potboiling in *Mike Fletcher*, which came out the following year, 1889. In his correspondence he enthusiastically referred to his "Don Juan book", and in the preface to *Spring Days* he disdainfully spoke of the dramatist, the librettist, and the poet who have given us for Don Juan "only a pretty boy with whom women fell in love". Mike Fletcher, we then might gather, was to be the fictional counterpart of the George Moore of the *Confessions*. To what extent would the Victorians allow George Moore to write "Don Juan"? This is an important question, for the answer tells whether the Victorians submerged and invalidated George Moore as a novelist during the years of Victoria's reign.

[3] *Spring Days*, London (Vizetelly) 1888.

Mike Fletcher is an anti-Victorian attempt. It ends dangerously close to being a Victorian novel. Mike himself is anti-Victorian. He is a writer for a weekly paper of modern tendencies, something of a poet, and a man whom women spontaneously like. He feels no responsibility for them, is carelessly amatory, and persuades a nun to leave a convent, without, however, going to bed with her. As a matter of fact, Mike doesn't really go to bed with anybody. He has *had* liaisons, but there is always some doubt of what happens in the present. He actually goes home with one woman, for several days in fact, and there is one mention that "she lay upon his knees in the black satin arm-chair" – but this seems rather cramped. We don't even see the two at breakfast, for "he was always strict in his own room". Mike inherits money from a former mistress. Later there is a gay party. Mike and fellow bohemians, male and female, decide to spend the week end at Brighton. Mike's girl friend is Kitty, a courtesan whose cut rate is twenty-five guineas, but who accepts no money from Mike. They all leave for Brighton, but Mike does not get there. He stops off on the way to have an intellectual conversation with a friend and neglects to join the party. Mike all the time has a real though unconsummated love – the girl whom he enticed from the nunnery. She is dying when Mike finally goes to the trouble of locating her. From this point on, I must confess, the story is a beautiful, mournful tone poem of the girl's death, Mike's sorrow, and his eventual suicide. The surrender to Nemesis is complete. Before his death Mike meditates: "For now I know that man cannot live without wife, without child, without God."

This Don Juan book is ruined by its evasions. Later in life George Moore could not bear to have *Mike Fletcher* mentioned. And the cause is not hard to find. Moore expressed it in 1906 in the preface to *Memoirs of My Dead Life*: "How false and shameful is the whole business. We are allowed to state that we prefer pagan morality to Christian, but are interdicted from illustrating our beliefs by incident. So long as we confine ourselves to theory we are unmolested."

We may pass hastily over George Moore's other Victorian writings. He returned to naturalistic material in *Esther Waters*, but his technique now involves a heroine and a happy ending, which makes it not naturalism at all. Moore was plainly disoriented and withal surprised at the success of *Esther Waters*. He stated that the return to a simple human theme in *Esther Waters* meant the end of his experimentation. Incidentally, Smith and Mudie had now capitulated. Yet he returned to experimentation and the abnormal when he took up again, in *Evelyn Innes*, 1898, and *Sister Teresa*, 1901, the sympathetic treatment of a religious theme – under Huysmans's influence, of course. Although *Evelyn Innes* is partly spoiled by its restraint and the frigid love affair, Moore's attempt had a sincere artistic motive. We recall that Moore once said, "A social or religious problem is as necessary to the realistic artist as disease is to a physician." A free treatment of social problems was forbidden him, so he turned to religious ones. Moore was gasping for air. And then, too, there was Huysmans.

I must add a word of caution. The thesis that George Moore was invalidated by Victorian reticence for nineteen years is altogether too simple. Moore was continuously in search of popularity and what his biographer calls a common notoriety. With an inherited income of £500 a year he did not need to write for money, yet he continually courted the patronage of Messrs Smith and Mudie and generally evinced a grasping nature. He was a poor judge of his own work, declaring his worst novel, *Spring Days*, the best thing he had written, and calling the almost prudish *Evelyn Innes* a powerful aphrodisiac. If he had been a greater man, and a greater writer, he would have compromised less. If he had been less great he would have shown less invention in trying to evade the Victorians. He would have been invalidated not merely for nineteen years, but longer. And, yes, he would have written more novels like *Esther Waters;* and I am personally pleased that he did not. His experimentation extended the range of the English novel.

William F. Blissett

GEORGE MOORE AND
LITERARY WAGNERISM[1]

George Moore mediated a great deal of the continental influence
on English literature in the last decades of the nineteenth century
and the first of the twentieth: but because of his habit of "studied
comicality" and his practice of self-denigration under the cover of
conceit, he has received small credit for his own originality and
his ability to pick winners. Among his "firsts", he led the way in
the writing of Wagnerian novels. Before Virginia Woolf in *The
Voyage Out* reported that Mrs Dalloway had heard *Parsifal* in
Bayreuth and swooned; before D. H. Lawrence in *The Trespasser*
made his Siegmund a violinist at Covent Garden, before Gertrude
Atherton and Willa Cather in *Tower of Ivory* and *The Song of the
Lark* recounted the life of American Wagnerian sopranos; before
Arnold Bennett in *Sacred and Profane Love* built the action of his
story round the seductive power of Tristan – George Moore had
written *Evelyn Innes* and its sequel *Sister Teresa*. Behind him lay
only Stanley Makower's rather slight *Mirror of Music* and E. F.
Benson's rather faint novelette, *The Rubicon*.[2]

[1] [Reprinted from *Comparative Literature*, XII (1961) pp. 52-71.]

[2] *The Voyage Out*, London (Duckworth) 1915; *The Trespasser*, London
(Duckworth) 1912; *Tower of Ivory*, London (Murray) 1910; *The Song of the
Lark*, Boston & N.Y. (Houghton Mifflin) 1915; *Sacred and Profane Love*,
London (Chatto & Windus) 1905; *Mirror of Music*, London, 1895; *The
Rubicon*, London, 1894. The two novels of Gabriele d'Annunzio most
saturated with Wagnerism, *Il trionfo della morte* (1894) and *Il fuoco* (1898), were
promptly translated into English (1896 and 1890) and enjoyed wide popularity.
Some aspects of English literary Wagnerism are treated by Max Moser in
Richard Wagner in der englischen Literatur des XIX. Jahrhunderts, Bern (1938);
Moore himself is discussed pp. 89-98.

Evelyn Innes opens at the end of a thin winter day to the sound of music played on the virginal. The novel appeared in 1898; the action may be placed in a vaguely defined time in the period when the English musical world's taste for Wagner was often combined with a taste for early music. Mr Innes, the organist of a Jesuit church in Dulwich, has given himself entirely to the cause of the old music, and we see him playing the "wailing chords" of Vittoria's motet *O Magnum Mysterium* and remarking to his daughter: "That is where Wagner went for his chorus of youth in the cupola. The critics haven't discovered it yet; they are still talking of Palestrina."[3]

That intelligent critic of music, James Gibbons Huneker, exclaimed in his review: "At last a novel with some intelligent criticism of music!"[4] Perhaps it is too early to recall Max Beerbohm's parody of George Moore in *A Christmas Garland*,[5] in which Moore meets Dolmetsch with a Mass by Palestrina under his arm. "Will you read me the score?" he asks, and Dolmetsch does, twice over. And yet it is surely literature and imperfectly remembered musical conversation that permitted Moore's Mr Innes to extract "wailing chords" from so unsonorous an instrument as the virginal or that prompted him to attempt to render a choral work in such a medium.

This, however, is background music in the novel. Evelyn has profited by her father's expert instruction in the technique and the chaste style of early church music, but has inherited the voice of her mother, who had been an opera singer. To the pair of them, sprouting despondently in Dulwich, there enters Sir Owen Asher, a rich musical dilettante who has heard of Mr Innes' efforts in the office of the *Wagnerian Review* and has hastened to investigate. Sir Owen is far gone in Wagnerism: "at five-and-thirty Bayreuth and its world of musical culture and ideas had interested him in spite of an unconquerable aversion to long hair and dirty hands".[6]

[3] *Evelyn Innes*, London (Fisher Unwin) 1898, p. 10.

[4] James G. Huneker, *Overtones*, New York (Scribners) 1904, p. 188.

[5] Max Beerbohm, *A Christmas Garland*, London (Heinemann) 1950, p. 177. Hardly less absurd is the passage in *Memoirs of my Dead Life*, London (Heinemann) revised edition 1915, p. 322, in which Moore asserts that he threw all his bank notes, gold and silver to a Bohemian fiddler bidding him "Give me *The Ring*, give me *The Ring*."

[6] *Evelyn Innes*, p. 13.

On hearing Evelyn sing at a concert of ancient music, he is struck by the Wagnerian timbre of her voice and decides to take the double chance of making her a Wagnerian singer and his mistress; to hear his creature sing Kundry at Bayreuth is his ultimate aim.

On one of his visits to Dulwich Sir Owen "was playing love music out of 'Tristan' on the harpsichord. The gnawing, creeping sensuality of the phrase brought little shudders into her flesh; all life seemed dissolved into a dim tremor and rustling of blood; vague colour floated into her eyes, and there were moments when she could hardly restrain herself from jumping to her feet and begging him to stop."[7] A curious passage: the idea of *Tristan* on the harpsichord is indubitably as creepy as the writer intends; and he gets the desired effect of an irruption of the sensual into the chaste, of the demands of the present into the arrangements of the past; and the description fits both Wagner and the harpsichord. The only snag is the practical impossibility of playing sustained groping oceanic harmonies on that instrument. Brilliant as metaphor, it is ludicrous as actuality.

With a little additional aid from Omar Khayyam, Théophile Gautier, and Herbert Spencer as solvents of morality, Sir Owen accomplishes his initial purpose. By a song from Purcell's *Indian Queen*, "at once religious and voluptuous, seemingly the rapture of a nun that remembrance has overtaken and for the moment overpowered",[8] Evelyn impresses a great teacher in Paris, and her career as an operatic singer is begun.

From that point, the novel is full of Wagnerian discussion, all of it topical in the heyday of English Wagnerism, and much of it skilfully integrated with the theme of the book and the life of its characters. Evelyn, for instance, is careful to differentiate between Isolde before and Isolde after she has drunk the love potion; the distinction is that between the daughter of Dulwich and the mistress of Covent Garden. Indeed, Sir Owen intended *Tristan and Isolde* to be his story and Evelyn's, but at the moment of fulfilment of her art and of their love Evelyn has a dream – she has the somnambulistic quality of the true Wagnerite. She dreams of two Tristans, a fair and a dark. The golden-whiskered rationalist Sir Owen is soon to have a rival, the Irish composer Ulick Dean, a dark-eyed occultist who could never have been conceived had not

[7] *Op. cit.*, p. 73.   [8] *Op. cit.*, p. 137.

a young Irish poet with raven forelock been known to Moore at the time.[9]

Sir Owen is an orthodox, Ulick a dissident Wagnerian. Ulick had "recanted his Wagnerian faith" in favour of a belief in the old gods of Ireland, and stood apart from that conflict of religion and sensuality within which Evelyn lived her life. Owen had very early formed the ambition to hear her sing Kundry, and on a journey up the Rhine had told her the story of *Parsifal*: but the meaning of the part then and later was to escape her, owing partly to the opinions of Ulick. Of Wagner's music dramas, Ulick deemed *Tannhäuser* to be perhaps the finest, being the sincerest, and *Parsifal* the worst, being the most hypocritical. Elisabeth was the essential penitent, she who does penance for the sins of others. Not for a moment could he admit the penitence of Kundry.[10] Ulick looks like a young W. B. Yeats, argues like a young D. H. Lawrence; he has the impatience of both with Evelyn's Roman Catholicism and Owen's dreary rationalism. The character of Parsifal he could admit even less than the character of Kundry. As he would say in vehement discussion:

> If I am to discuss an artistic question, I must go to the very heart of it. Now, if we ask ourselves what Siegfried did, the answer is, that he forged the sword, killed the dragon and released Brünnhilde. But if, in like manner, we ask ourselves what Parsifal did, is not the answer, that he killed a swan and refused a kiss and with many morbid, suggestive and disagreeable remarks?[11]

Wagner, he says, had long been considering an opera with a subjective hero – Christ or Buddha; when into a pretty medieval myth he had shot the material gathered for greater subjects, the old wine burst the new bottle. Besides, "in neither Christ nor Buddha did the question of sex arise, and that was the reason that Wagner eventually rejected them both. He was as full of

[9] *Op. cit.*, pp. 152, 265, 276, 153, 151. In the 1901 revision of the novel Ulick ceases to resemble Yeats and takes on the features of A.E. An Irish episode is added in which Evelyn and her lover visit Chapelizod, the legendary home of Isolde.

[10] *Op. cit.*, pp. 68-9, 159, 179, 281, 284, 192.

[11] *Op. cit.*, p. 193.

sex – mysterious, subconscious sex – as Rossetti himself." And he concludes concerning *Parsifal*, adumbrating from his oblique position the religious theme of the novel as it is to work itself out: "The airs of this mock redeemer were truly unbearable, and the abjection of Kundry before this stuffed Christ revolted him." Late in the book, with Evelyn abject before him, Monsignor Mostyn strangely echoes these views: *Parsifal*, he tells his penitent, is a parody of the Mass, whether performed at Bayreuth or elsewhere.[12]

Not only does Evelyn sing and discuss Wagner, she is caught in a swirl of Wagnerian situations. When she goes off with Sir Owen, she recognises her father in Wotan as she sings the role of the disobedient Brünnhilde, and she often tries to work out the allegory, but lacks the energy and clarity of mind. Again, Ulick and Evelyn recognise their story in *Tristan*; Evelyn is carried by the music and by "currents of the blood" into yielding, and it is as if she had taken of the love potion; the end is described as nervous exhaustion. If Ulick is Tristan, Mr Innes and Owen share the character of Marke: but again the resemblance is allowed to dissolve.[13] George Moore uses Wagnerian parallels as often as James Joyce was to use Homeric parallels but without Joyce's appearance of system.

One thing, however, is kept in focus and that is the opposition of Wagner and Catholicism as correlatives of Evelyn's state of sin and state of grace. Everything before Wagner seems to her "like a pious book"; Catholicism seems exoteric and insufficient – like Gounod. True, the first step in Evelyn's conversion is a Wagner-ian concert in aid of her old convent, a concert at which "every degree of Wagner culture was present, from the ten-antlered stag who had seen 'Parsifal' given under the eye of the master to the skipping fawns eagerly browsing upon the motives".[14] But the sisters of the convent are not there; and, when Evelyn is drawn closer to them, her opulent voice – made so by Wagner – is incongruous and disturbing. She gives much thought to the penitent roles in Wagner; and when she is Owen's mistress she can also be the medieval virgin Elisabeth: but Kundry she is never

---

[12] *Op. cit.*, pp. 194, 195, 333.
[13] *Op. cit.*, pp. 203, 212, 239, 264, 277, 299, 362, 389.
[14] *Op. cit.*, pp. 301, 342, 343.

to be, on the stage or off it, for Monsignor Mostyn puts an end to Wagnerian role playing, to idolatry, hypocrisy, and sensual drift.

George Moore is not reputed to be a particularly improving writer, and a reader of *Evelyn Innes* may be surprised at his grip on moral fact. It would have been fatally easy to have allowed any one or a combination of the specific Wagnerian parallels to force the characters and the action rigidly in a given direction. Instead, the theme (which is, to be sure, not foreign to Wagner) of the conflict and combination of religion and sensuality imposes its own unity on the material, so that Evelyn's conversion and her attendant renunciation of the stage is at the end inevitable and right.

The reappraisal in *Sister Teresa* is likewise inevitable. Evelyn "had discovered two instincts in herself, an inveterate sensuality and a sincere aspiration for a spiritual life"; no sooner has she renounced the first in the interest of the second than she experiences "a third revelation – that the sexual trouble was but the surface of her nature, that beyond it there was a deeper nature whose depths were yet unsounded". Unsounded they remain. *Sister Teresa* is inferior in interest to *Evelyn Innes*, the ebbing of hope, the note of regret, the dying fall, cannot sustain a whole book. There is, however, one passage of power and terror, in which Sister Teresa suffers a nightmare. She is playing Brünn-hilde and lies on the mountain top surrounded by the magic fire. The hero forces his way to her, and "she heard her vows die as Siegfried's lips pressed hers apart". Awake, "she lay quiescent, and her whole life seemed to be read out to her, and at the end of the long reading she answered, 'No Siegfried will come to release me from this prision of invisible bars. And if Siegfried came to release me from these flames – for every will is a flame – of what use should I be to him?' "[15] That is the last gleam at the end of Evelyn Innes' thin winter day.

How did George Moore come to write a book so saturated with Wagner? To say that Wagner was a topic of the day is true but

---

[15] *Sister Teresa*, London (Unwin) 1901, pp. 8, 199, 200. Moore was never to rest content with *Evelyn Innes* and its sequel, in any version, and concluded finally, though perhaps unfairly, that "a superficial subject had better be written superficially". "Apologia pro Scriptis meis", *Fortnightly Review*, cxii (1922), pp. 536-7.

not sufficient, for Moore himself had long been, in his own phrase, "rotten with Wagnerism", and in this he was near the forefront of English fashion, not a follower.

Young George Moore left bucolic Ireland in 1870, and we may suppose that he was at the time as innocent as his friend Mr Ryan was to be, who saw a photograph of Wagner on the club table and asked, "Who is that?"

> I: That is Wagner.
>
> Mr Ryan: Who is Wagner?
>
> I (recovering myself with an effort): Don't you know? Richard Wagner, the great breeder of short horns!
>
> Mr Ryan: Begorra 'tis strange I never came across him in Ballinasloe . . .[16]

In 1873 Moore settled in Paris, on the Quai Voltaire, but the fact that Wagner had stayed there while writing *Die Meistersinger* seems not to have registered on him at the time. With a sublime, a Wagnerian, egotism the young lover and consumer busies himself in collecting and discarding books and friends and equipping himself for his double role, "the youngest of the naturalists and the eldest of the symbolists". His shadow lengthens a generation into the future, and we discern Stephen Dedalus collecting epiphanies and J. M. Synge listening to the Aran Islanders through a chink in the floor as Moore recounts how "with the patience of a cat before a mouse-hole, I watched and listened, picking one characteristic phrase out of hours of vain chatter, interested and amused by an angry or loving glance".[17]

He was just as selectively sensitive to the ideas current in the world of the arts. Professor Malcolm Brown asks: "How many readers owe their discovery of Balzac, Flaubert, Zola, Turgenev, Huysmans, Verlaine, Monet, Degas, and even Wagner to the infectiousness of Moore's enthusiasms?"[18] It is right to say "even Wagner", to put the composer in a special category; for what

---

[16] *Parnell and his Island*, London, 1887, pp. 18-19.

[17] *Memoirs of my Dead Life*, London (Heinemann), 1906, p. 48; *Confessions of a Young Man*, London (Heinemann), 1937, pp. 19, 22 – this was the final version published in the Ebury edition.

[18] Malcolm Brown, *George Moore: A Reconsideration*, Seattle (University of Washington Press), p. xii.

Moore discovered and communicated in his Paris phase was not Wagner himself and his music – that was to come later – but French literary Wagnerism. This fact is proclaimed throughout the *Confessions of a Young Man*. For instance, it is when Moore is discussing not music but poetry, not Wagner but Mallarmé, that he remarks of *L'Après-midi d'un faune* that it bears the same relation to the author's later work as *Rienzi* does to *Die Walküre*; and the ensuing discussion of symbolism in poetry could have been written by a man who had never heard a note of Wagner – but had puzzled over Mallarmé's sonnet, "Hommage à Richard Wagner".[19]

Of one of Verlaine's poems he writes: "The charm is that of an odour of iris exhaled by some ideal tissues, or of a missal in a gold case, a precious relic of the pomp and ritual of an archbishop of Persepolis."[20] An anticipation of the literary tone of the 'nineties? True. But the poem in question is Verlaine's "Parsifal". Like Mallarmé's poem, this appeared in the *Revue Wagnérienne*.

One of the most vivid portraits of a French man of letters in the *Confessions* is that of Catulle Mendès:

> a perfect realization of his name, with his pale hair, and his fragile face illuminated with the idealism of a depraved woman. He takes you by the arm, by the hand, he leans toward you, his words are caresses, his fervour is delightful, and to hear him is as sweet as drinking a smooth perfumed wine. All he says is false – the book he has just read, the play he is writing, the woman who loves him . . . He buys a packet of bonbons in the streets and eats them, and it is false.

The book that Catulle Mendès had just read when Moore knew him might have been one of his own, on Wagner, or of his wife, Judith Gautier, on Wagner, or of their friend Villiers de l'Isle Adam, with whom they visited Wagner in Triebschen on their way to hear the premières of *Das Rheingold* and *Die Walküre* in Munich.[21]

---

[19] *Confessions of a Young Man*, p. 49.

[20] *Op. cit.*, p. 52.

[21] *Op. cit.*, p. 48. See Catulle Mendès, *Richard Wagner* (1886); Judith Gautier, *Richard Wagner et son œuvre poétique* (1882); Villiers de l'Isle Adam,

The one person from this milieu who remained a lifelong friend of Moore's was Edouard Dujardin. Dujardin had received some musical education and was blessed with a small talent as a critic and writer and a considerable talent as an editor and publicist. After conversations in Munich with Houston Stewart Chamberlain he had returned to Paris to edit the *Revue Wagnérienne* (1883-6), the literary organ, simultaneously and equally, of Wagnerism and symbolism. It was he who used to take Mallarmé to "Vespers" – the Wagner concerts on Sunday evenings – and even when the interests of this boulevardier and speculator on the financial and literary markets turned to Christian origins (as Moore's also was to turn), he remained a faithful if not a fanatical Wagnerite and a frequent pilgrim to Bayreuth. Today he is chiefly remembered because James Joyce told a reporter after the publication of *Ulysses* that he had taken the idea of the interior monologue from a novel of Dujardin's, *Les Lauriers sont coupés*. Not many recall the postscript to the story – that Dujardin, summoned like Lazarus back into the land of the living, explained that his technique had been devised in an attempt to achieve in literature the effect of Wagnerian music.[22]

There is no evidence that Dujardin succeeded in communicating his enthusiasm for Wagner's music dramas to Moore during the Paris years: but there is in the *Confessions* (removed from the editions after 1888) an indication that Moore was already saturated in Wagnerian literary ideas of the sort that Dujardin was active in propagating, and that he had already conceived the idea of what was to be his own late style, and conceived it in Wagnerian terms.

Contes cruels (1883). See also Judith Gautier, *Auprès de Richard Wagner: Souvenirs (1861-82)* (1943); G. Jean-Aubrey, "Villiers de l'Isle Adam and Music", *Music and Letters*, xix (1938), pp. 391-404; Kurt Jäckel, *Richard Wagner in der französischen Literatur*, Breslau (1931-2) I, pp. 103-4, II, pp. 11-23, 24-40.

[22] Dujardin's novel, Paris (1888) has been translated by Stuart Gilbert as *We'll to the Woods No More*, New York (New Directions) 1938. Dujardin's place in French Wagnerism is discussed by Jäckel, *op. cit.*, II, pp. 49-53. See also Aristide Marie, *La Forêt symboliste*, Paris (Firmin-Didot) 1936, Ch. III on Dujardin, Ch. IV on Moore; and Jacques-Emile Blanche, *Portraits of a Lifetime*, tr. Walter Clement, London (Dent) 1937, pp. 84-7. For Dujardin's acknowledgment of Wagner's influence on his technique, see *Le Monologue intérieur*, Paris (Messein) 1931, pp. 54-5, 58, 104.

Apropos of *Lorna Doone*, which struck him as no better than a third-rate Italian opera, he wrote:

> Wagner made the discovery, not a very wonderful one after all when we think, that an opera had much better be melody from beginning to end. The realistic school following on Wagner's footsteps discovered that a novel had much better be all narrative – an uninterrupted flow of narrative. Description is narrative, analysis of character is narrative, dialogue is narrative; the form is ceaselessly changing, but the melody of narration is never interrupted.[23]

George Moore's Wagnerism is already complete in Paris, but empty as yet of Wagner.

Gradually Wagner came to figure, as topic and influence, in Moore's early art – taking *Evelyn Innes* as the dividing line between early and late. Certain passages in the earliest novels, not quoted here,[24] are so many missed opportunities; in them, Wagner is a filler or at best a dash of colour. And then suddenly, quite late in the development of a rather lack-lustre realistic novel, *Spring Days* (1888), an experience of *Tristan and Isolde* forces its way through the surface of the book, and we are embarrassingly confronted with this:

[23] *Confessions of a Young Man*, 2nd edn., London (1888), pp. 270-1. Omitted from later editions. The passage on Zola's *Assommoir* is concerned with the same technical question, as Professor Brown points out in *George Moore*, p. 182.

[24] See *Lewis Seymour and Some Women* (revision of *A Modern Lover*) London (Heinemann) 1917, p. 30; *A Modern Lover*, 2nd edn., London (Tinsley) 1885, pp. 41, 124; *A Mummer's Wife*, London (Heinemann) 1936 (this is the final – 1918 – version) p. 241; *A Mere Accident*, London (1887); *Mike Fletcher*, London (1889), pp. 126-7. Further incidental references to Wagner and Wagnerism are to be found in *Conversations in Ebury Street*, London (Heinemann) 1930, pp. 10, 131, 162ff., 234, 237; *Avowals*, London (Heinemann) 1924, pp. 10, 130, 193, 236; *Impressions and Opinions*, London (1891), pp. 280-1; and in the prefaces to his plays, *Esther Waters*, London (Heinemann) 1913, pp. xi, xiv; and *The Coming of Gabrielle*, London (Society for Irish Folklore) 1920, pp. xxii, xxvii-xxviii. For Wagnerism in the letters, see John Eglinton, ed. and tr., *Letters from George Moore to Ed. Dujardin, 1886-1922*, New York (Crosby Gaige) 1929, *passim*, especially pp. 20, 43-4, 73. See also Rupert Hart-Davis, ed., *George Moore: Letters to Lady Cunard, 1895-1933*, London (Hart-Davis) 1957, pp. 21, 25, 40, 62ff., 84; Nancy Cunard, *G. M.: Memoirs of George Moore*, London (Hart-Davis) 1956, pp. 43, 46, 52, 74-5.

The lovers have drunk of the magic philtre, their bowels are full of love; their brains are aflame with love; they have striven, they have resisted, they are now weary and flesh-sore. They are alone – alone and facing the beautiful night. Too weary are they of the day that separates them, and they are fearful of life that will punish them for too great happiness. "Descend upon us, night of love, give me forgetfulness of life, gather me to thy breast, take me across this universe. Already the last lights are retiring; that which we thought we saw, remembrances and images of things, the remains of illusion, august presentiments of the holy darkness, extinguish all in taking us across the world. As soon as the sun has set in our breasts, the stars of happiness shall spread their laughing light. The world and paling fascination, the world that the moon lights with her deceitful beams, the false sceptre that the day places before me; it is I who am the world. Live holy love, august offspring of voluptuousness, delicious desire of eternal sleep, without form and unawakening " Faint and intermittent memories of the music came to him as he stood on the dock.[25]

The rudderless skiff of Moore's prose enters the Wagnerian whirl-pool.

At this juncture George Moore left the centre of literary Wag-nerism, and later London, the centre of what may be called social Wagnerism (the Wagnerism of society and of socialism), for his native Ireland. Some account of the relation of Wagner to the Irish literary revival is in order. I believe that the influence is considerable, though much mediated and combined with other currents of thought. If W. B. Yeats had not happened to be tone-deaf! . . .

Bernard Shaw did not take all the Wagnerism of Ireland with him to London; indeed it is odd that the heir of the intellectual tradition of comedy should have been a Wagnerite at all.[26] Those of the next generation who stayed in Ireland and tried to re-establish its heroic tradition were far more ready seed ground for

[25] *Spring Days*, London, 1888, pp. 313-14. Removed after the first edition.
[26] William Blissett, "Bernard Shaw Imperfect Wagnerite", *University of Toronto Quarterly*, XVII (1958), pp. 185-99.

Wagner the mythologist of national origins.[27] And, when Irish literary development turned decisively toward the drama, it so happened that the Irishman and the Englishwoman who share much of the credit, financial and otherwise, for making an independent theatre possible in Ireland – Edward Martyn and Miss Horniman – were both fervent Wagnerites.[28] Moore's friend for many years, Martyn, came under Wagner's spell while at Oxford, went often to Bayreuth, sometimes in Moore's company, and devoted his riches and talents to the establishment of a Palestrina Choir in Dublin Cathedral and to the writing and production of plays in which Ibsen is the primary but Wagner a secondary influence. Martyn may well have had firsthand knowledge of all the independent theatres of Europe – Wagner's in Bayreuth (1876), Antoine's in Paris (1887), Brahms' in Berlin (1889), Grein's in London (1891), his own Irish Literary Theatre in Dublin (1899), and its successor, Miss Horniman's Irish National Theatre (1904). Miss Horniman, the Manchester spinster of ample means who supplied the Irish dramatists with the Abbey Theatre, was likewise a Wagnerite from her youth up. Not only was she a regular pilgrim to Bayreuth, which must to her as to Martyn have been the archetype of the art theatre, but she helped her friend Ashton Ellis in his labours of translating

[27] Standish O'Grady's histories and collection of Irish heroic legends began to appear in 1878; T. W. Rolleston's *Myths and Legends of the Celtic Race* was published in 1911 but was preceded by *Imagination and Art in Gaelic Literature* in 1900. Rolleston was a strong Wagnerite. Among historians of the Irish movement, Ernest A. Boyd in *Ireland's Literary Renaissance*, New York (Maunsel) 1916, p. 117, pointed out the resemblance of the story of Cuchulain and Fand to Venus and Tannhäuser; Dawson Byrne in *The Story of Ireland's National Theatre*, Dublin (1929), quoted Wagner as an epigraph in his foreword; and T. C. Murray in Lennox Robinson's collection, *The Irish Theatre*, London (Macmillan), 1939, wrote: "In the rich mine of Celtic myth and legend there lay at hand, they believed, a wealth of material which needed only the instinct of the dramatist to re-create it in the form demanded by the stage. It was no illogical theory, for such national legendary lore had been the main source not only of the dramatic literature of Ancient Greece but of Ibsen's *Peer Gynt* and *Brand* and the splendid music-drama of Wagner" (p. 120).

[28] Denis Gwynn, *Edward Martyn and the Irish Revival*, London (Cape) 1930; Sister Mary Courtney, *Edward Martyn*, New York (Vantage Press) 1956; Rex Pogson, *Miss Horniman*, London (Rockliff) 1952; see also references to Miss Horniman's Wagnerism in Allan Wade, ed., *The Letters of W. B. Yeats*, London (Hart-Davis) 1954, p. 262, note 2, p. 371, note 3, pp. 459-60.

Wagner's prose works and editing *The Meister*, the periodical of the English Wagner Society. She and Ellis, like so many other Wagnerites in France, England, and the United States, were theosophists; and so Wagner, literally, exercised an occult influence.[29]

Ireland developed its own musical tradition based on operatic arias and sentimental ballads, and *Dubliners* and *Ulysses* show us how expressive it could be. Shaw's is a minority voice: "It is an Irish defect to lose grip and interest by neglecting the words – thinking only of the music. Cats do the same thing when they are serenading one another; but the genuineness of their emotion gives them poignancy."[30] Irish singers in drawing rooms, concert rooms, and pubs – Molly Bloom, and Simon Dedalus – were not usually of Wagnerian stuff, and the literary movement was not at first strong enough to dictate musical taste.

A chronicler of this tradition, John Todhunter, born in 1839, lived long enough to sigh for a Wagnerian opera without vocal parts.[31] (Did he not get it in the tragedies of Yeats and Synge?) Out of sympathy though he was with Wagnerian music, he had himself written a *Rienzi* in 1881; and after his death in 1916 his *Isolt of Ireland* was published, proving that a literary affinity with Wagner can survive a musical antipathy.

The first Irish writer in whom musical and literary Wagnerism were to be combined was T. W. Rolleston. During his years in Germany, in which he came to know Wagner's works, he became adept enough in German to translate *Leaves of Grass*; and in letters

[29] Sar Peladan, the Rosicrucian, and Edouard Schuré, the follower of Rudolf Steiner, were among the leading French translators and commentators on Wagner; a perusal of the theosophist journals of London, Dublin, and New York discloses that far more attention was devoted to the message of Wagner than to that of any other modern artist. See especially *The Grail*, London (1897), I, p. 3, II, pp. 32-3, V, pp. 134-6; *The Internationalist*, Dublin (1897), continued as *The International Theosophist*, Dublin (1898-1904), which has some dozen Wagner extracts or articles.

[30] Clifford Bax, ed., *Florence Farr, Bernard Shaw, W. B. Yeats, Letters*, New York (Dodd, Mead) 1942, pp. 22-3, a letter dated 6 Jun. 1902.

[31] John Todhunter, *Essays*, London (Elkin Mathews) 1920, pp. 170-1. Frances Gerard, who wrote books on *Celebrated Irish Beauties*, London, 1895, and *Picturesque Dublin*, London, 1898, also produced popular works on *The Romance of King Ludwig II of Bavaria*, London, 1899, and *Wagner, Bayreuth, and the Festival Plays*, London (Jarrold) 1901.

to Whitman he found affinities between the musician and the poet. Later he wrote verse himself, and was in the chair at meetings of the Rymers' Club and represented in both its collections. His Irish and his Wagnerian enthusiasms were concurrent. At the same time that he was writing *The High Deeds of Finn* (1910) and *Myths & Legends of the Celtic Race* (1911), he produced translations of *Lohengrin* (1911) and *Tannhäuser* (1912) and a free paraphrase of *Parsifal* (1913) for editions sumptuously decorated by Willy Pógany.[32] When he came to collect them, he found that the title he wished to use – *Sacred and Profane Love* – had already been appropriated by Arnold Bennett, for a Wagnerian novel!

George Moore dedicated the first edition of *Evelyn Innes* "to Arthur Symons and W. B. Yeats, Two Contemporary Writers with whom I am in sympathy". Moore followed Yeats back to their native land, and Symons too was to discover that he was a Celt and to visit Ireland in 1896 and in the early years of the new century, to the delight of the young intellectuals whose darling he was.[33] Symons was perhaps the most influential critic of his day, and played a part equal to Moore's own in mediating French influence in the English-speaking world. And, as in Moore's case, his musical Wagnerism developed from literature. He possessed Swinburne's copy of Baudelaire's essay, "Richard Wagner et Tannhäuser à Paris", the premier document of literary Wagnerism; he knew – personally in some cases – the Wagnerites Verlaine, Mallarmé, Huysmans, D'Annunzio. As editor of the *Savoy* he published Aubrey Beardsley's Tannhäuser pastiche, "Under the Hill", and made preliminary arrangements for the serial appearance of *Evelyn Innes*. In 1899 he published in *The Dome* his own highly perceptive essay on "Parsifal".[34]

We may imagine how pervasive if not how explicit would be the Wagnerism of the conversations of Lady Gregory and Yeats at Coole and of Moore, Martyn, and Symons at near-by Tillyra.

[32] The texts were collected, without the decorations, as *Three Love Tales*, London (Harrap) 1920.

[33] Mary Colum, *Life and the Dream*, London (Macmillan) 1947, p. 121.

[34] Arthur Symons, *Charles Baudelaire*, London (Elkin Mathews) 1920, pp. 101-2; "Bayreuth: Notes on Wagner", *The Dome*, IV (1898) pp. 145-9. In a letter to Symons (10 Sep. 1905) Yeats praised an essay of Symons on "The Ideas of Richard Wagner", written in 1905, and included in *Studies in Seven Arts*, London (Archibald Constable) 1906; *Letters*, pp. 459-60.

Indeed, in the writings of the tone-deaf Yeats alone there is ample material for such a surmise. In his discussions with John Eglinton in defence of national as against cosmopolitan literature, Yeats appeals to the example of Wagner, who successfully returned to national origins and mythical subjects, and clearly he sees himself as doing the same sort of thing for Ireland. All his incidental references to Wagner are favourable; what he would like is an Irish literary Bayreuth.[35]

When Moore and Yeats were very close, they collaborated in writing the play, *Diarmuid and Grania*, which is more like Wagner and less like Ibsen than any previous work for the Irish theatre. Edward Martyn had led the way with *The Heather Field* and *Maeve* (1899), the latter being a play with Celtic twilight laid on like eye shadow, in which the present-day action recedes into the mythical patterns of Irish antiquity. The first and more successful was more Ibsen-like in theme – turning on the certification of an impractical idealist by the crass practicality of the world and of woman – but more Wagnerian in its references; for early in the action the hero recalls to his young brother their trip on the Rhine and their fanciful thoughts of river nymphs and river gold, and, mad at the end of the play, he exclaims: "Oh, we must go to

[35] John Eglinton, W. B. Yeats, A. E., W. Larminie, *Literary Ideals of Ireland*, London (1899), pp. 17-19 (Yeats), pp. 24-5 (Eglinton); John Eglinton, *Pebbles from a Brook*, Kilkenny (Standish O'Grady) 1901, p. 25; W. B. Yeats, *A Book of Images*, London (1898), pp. 10-12; *Essays* (1924), pp. 229-31, 331: but in the introduction to Pound's translation of *Certain Noble Plays of Japan*, Dundrum (Cuala Press) 1916, Yeats appears to be in reaction against Wagnerism in his reference to "bodily distance, mechanism and loud noise" (p. v). Gerald Fay in his study of *The Abbey Theatre*, London (Hollis) 1958, quotes a letter from Frank Fay to Yeats: "I know what Wagner did and what Antoine has done, but they were both men of irresistible genius and nature had given them the fighting qualities that would enable them to do their work. Besides they lived in countries vastly different from Ireland where the majority are willing slaves. I find myself continually saying 'Oh that the Irish Literary Theatre had built a hall!' " (p. 41). To this Yeats replied (21 Apr. 1902): "Now as to the future of the National Theatre Company, I read your letters to a wealthy friend who said something like this: Work on as best you can for a year, let us say, you should be able to persuade people during that time that you are something of a dramatist and Mr Fay should be able to have got a little practice for his company. At the year's end do what Wagner did and write a 'letter to my Friends' asking for the capital to carry out your idea" (p. 42).

the Lorlei [sic] as last year, where the river is lit by their gold. See, even now the sky is darkening as in that storm scene of the old legend I told you on the Rhine. See, the rain across a saffron sun trembles like gold harp strings, through the purple Irish spring!"[36] The Ludwig II of the Western World goes off the Wagnerian ravings (certainly Martyn is, as the young Joyce observed, "disabled by an incorrigible style"),[37] and the play closes, as does *Das Rheingold*, with music and a rainbow.

Diarmuid and Grania was finished in the year after Martyn's plays and was performed in October 1901.[38] Both Moore in *Ave* and Yeats in the *Autobiographies* give accounts of its composition and of the friction attendant on their division of labour – Moore was to supply the dramatic fable and the dialogue, Yeats the final poetic rendering. Yeats writes of Moore:

> He would have been a master of contruction, but that his practice as a novelist made him long for descriptions and reminiscences. If *Diarmuid and Grania* failed in performance, and I am not sure that it did, it failed because the second act, instead of moving swiftly from incident to incident, was reminiscent and descriptive; almost a new first act.[39]

The play is full of Wagnerian motifs accommodated to Irish legend. Grania's mother is something of a Norn; Diarmuid has attributes of Siegfried. Grania, to be sure, is no model of constancy, and the final speech by the churl, Conan, ends the play on a quite un-Wagnerian note: "Grania makes great mourning for Diarmuid, but her welcome to Finn shall be greater." There is a point of contact with the Wagnerian heroines nonetheless, which is brought out by the observation that Grania (like Elsa and Elisabeth, like Brünnhilde and Kundry) "was not meant to sit by the fireside with children on her knees. The gods made her womb barren because she was not meant to hold children on her knees.

[36] Edward Martyn, *The Heather Field and Maeve*, London (1899), p. 83.

[37] *The Critical Writings of James Joyce*, eds., Ellsworth Mason and Richard Ellman, London (Faber) 1959, p. 71.

[38] "Diarmuid and Grania. A Play in Three Acts", ed. William Becker, *Dublin Magazine*, XXVI (1951) pp. 1-41. We recall that Ulick Dean's post-Wagnerian opera in *Evelyn Innes* was on this theme. For the play, incidental music was provided by Sir Edward Elgar.

[39] W. B. Yeats, *Autobiographies*, London (Macmillan) 1955, p. 436.

The gods gave her a barren womb, hungry and barren like the sea.
She looked from the red apple in her hand to the green apple on
the bough." The style, a deliberate and sophisticated attempt to
employ incremental repetition of primitive narrative, is Wagnerian in its "endlessness", its progress by repetition and modifica-
tion of phrase; and this Wagnerian characteristic, seen in the
larger elements of construction, may be what Yeats is complaining
of. As Joseph Hone remarks of the collaborators, "The one
hankered after a Grania of folk and the other imagined a play in
the style of *Die Walküre* or *Tristan und Isolde*."[40]

At the time that Moore was concerned with the Irish theatre
(and inwardly detaching himself from Irish literature and politics),
he was also writing two works of fiction set in Ireland; his
Wagnerian preoccupation shows in both. *The Untilled Field* does
for Ireland what *Dubliners* was to do for the city; one is the
periphery, the other the centre of paralysis. In it the sound of a
shepherd's pipe in the mist is taken as symbolic of Irish soul-
sickness and melancholy; and, if one is reminded of the shepherd's
mournful tune in the third act of *Tristan*, this is probably not
counter to Moore's intention.[41] That was in 1903; in 1905
appeared a novel, *The Lake*, of which the author thought very
highly. In it an Irish parish priest, a man of unusual sensitivity as
well as force of character, leaves holy orders for the love of a
woman whom he had earlier driven out of his parish. His conscience had been disturbed by his own rigorism, and he and Rose
Leicester enter into a correspondence in which solicitude ripens
into friendship and into love. Rose is musical and goes to

---

[40] Joseph Hone, *The Life of George Moore*, London (Gollancz) 1936, p. 238.
Lennox Robinson similarly observed: "The play is colourful, full of ghosts
and hag-ridden people; the last act, painting a wonderful picture of wind and
storm, crashing trees, thunder and lightning, reminds one of a Wagnerian
opera – Moore's work perhaps?" *Ireland's Abbey Theatre*, London (Sidgwick
& Jackson) 1951, p. 21. It was not a success; perhaps it was of this play that
Eglinton was thinking when he wrote that "the heroic element seemed a little
crestfallen on the Abbey stage, and the Irish heroes, impersonated by actors
who had gained their renown in peasant parts, gave one the feeling that they
had fallen on very evil times, especially when one thought of their Teutonic
composers, moving amid the splendours of Wagnerian orchestration".
Irish Literary Portraits, London (Macmillan) 1935, p. 30.

[41] *The Untilled Field*, London (Fisher Unwin) 1903, pp. 323, 388-90, 417.

Munich for Mozart and to Bayreuth for Wagner. In one of her letters she writes to Father Gogarty (the name though not the character is taken from a young medical man and writer whom Moore knew) about "how the Rhine reminds one of Time. How many thousand years has the Rhine flowed! Just as it flowed the day we were at Bopart it was flowing when Wotan was God, and there were nymphs in the Rhine watching the gold, the innocent gold, that Alberich stole from them and converted into money."[42] And thus a second time Moore makes Wagner the opposite pole to the doctrine and discipline of the Catholic Church.

Each phase of Moore's life and writing is marked by efforts in drama, fiction, and autobiographical rumination. In the last category are his unclouded successes; and his Irish period produced one of the great autobiographies of our literature – *Hail and Farewell*. Naturally, one expects and finds Wagner massively present as a topic and as part of the stuff of experience: but the Wagnerian influence is more pervasive than that. *Hail and Farewell* has a thematic unity no less than the novels – in fact, it makes a fuller and more perceptive exploration of lifelong preoccupation with religious sensuality than any other of Moore's works.

The work is a trilogy introduced by what Moore calls an "overture", a passage of about thirty pages that sets the mood and sounds some of the themes of the book but does not anticipate its action – in short, a Wagnerian prelude analogous to the opening sections of those other Wagnerian works of literature, Proust's *A la recherche du temps perdu* and Thomas Mann's *Joseph* saga.

Thereafter occur some incidental Wagner references, of small moment except to show the interests of Moore's friends and the

---

[42] *The Lake*, London (Heinemann) 1905, pp. 147, 173-89. Wagner figures as more than a topic in *The Lake*; in a letter to Lady Cunard (Aug. 1905) Moore says, "It is my landscape book – and some of the landscape is a memory of the forest. 'The forest is like a harp', the breeze lifts the branches and a bird sings: a touch of art was added to the vague murmur I hear and the Siegfried music was made" (p. 45). And later, in "The Nineness in the Oneness", *Century Magazine*, n. s., LXXVII (1919), p. 66, he writes: " 'Evelyn Innes' is externally musical as 'Carmen' is externally Spanish; but the writing of 'The Lake' would not be as it is if I had not listened to 'Lohengrin' many times ... the pages in which the agitated priest wanders about a summer lake recall the silver of the prelude. The sun shining on the mist, a voice ... heard in vibrant supplication, is the essence of the prelude ..."

natural way in which Wagnerian allusions spring to his mind. The middle of the first volume, however, is dominated by an account of a journey to Bayreuth, in the course of which Moore "fell to thinking of the extraordinary joy and interest that Bayreuth had been in my life ever since Edward [Martyn] and I went there for the first time, after hearing a performance of the *Ring* in London. It had been the horns announcing the Rhine that re-awakened my musical conscience."[43] They make their pilgrimage and are received graciously by Cosima and Siegfried. Was Bayreuth worth the journey? "The answer made to this – and it was a woman who made it – was that the journey would be more real in six months time than it was today, and picking up the thought, I answered quickly: So you think that we live not so much for the moment as for the sake of the memory of it."[44] This Proustian comment, seemingly so casual, indicates perhaps that Moore (like Arthur Symons) has surmounted one of the first obstacles to the comprehension of Wagner and has seen that the extended passages of reminiscence in the *Ring* are not excrescences or *longueurs* but essential reinterpretations of experience.

Moore travelled to hear *Parsifal* in the company of Parsifal. We recall from *Evelyn Innes* the outspoken attack on that one of all Wagner's dramas by Ulick Dean, a character modelled in the first edition on Yeats, in the second on A.E., but a spokesman on musical matters, one would surmise, for Moore himself. That is the only Wagnerian opinion in the novel that could not have been derived from Edward Martyn.[45] Here again in *Hail and Farewell*, *Parsifal* is found not to be presonally appealing. But Edward Martyn, who by a miracle of playful affection on Moore's part becomes more and more personally appealing as the book progresses, is presented throughout as a Parsifal, a pure fool, a gooseless gander.

Both sides of Martyn's nature – the downright peasant stock of his mother and the Martyns, "the Parsifal side", with their

---

[43] *Hail and Farewell, Ave*, London (Heinemann) 1947 (final version) pp. 126-69, especially p. 151.

[44] *Op. cit.*, p. 165.

[45] *Hail and Farewell, Salve*, London (Heinemann) 1947 (final version) p. 94. Martyn wrote an article on "Wagner's Parsifal, or the Cult of Liturgical Aestheticism" in the *Irish Review*, III (1913) pp. 535-40.

ancient tradition of religious chivalry – seemed to destine Edward
for the priesthood. Instead, after leaving Oxford, he devoted his
time, fortune, and talents to Wagner, to the reform of church
music, and to the Irish cause in literature and in politics. He
remained devout all his life but was as obstinate as his mother,
and resolutely set his face against both marriage and holy orders.
Martyn had already provided Moore with the recurring character
John Norton in some earlier works, but Norton is a mere stick of
a celibate and remains dead on the page. In *Hail and Farewell*
Martyn comes alive under his own name in all his pure foolishness.
Like many confessions of love, this can be – has been – mistaken
for its opposite.

When Edward lived in Ely Place, Moore used to whistle a motif
from the *Ring* to summon him; and, if Edward in his limitations
is associated with *Parsifal*, a work that must be borne for Wagner's
sake, Moore comes increasingly to associate himself with the true
and essential Wagner, the Wagner of *Siegfried* – for we learn in the
third part that the password motif is Siegfried's. What this means
in the design of the whole trilogy is disclosed near the end, when
Moore, having given an account first of his political conversion
to the Irish cause and then of his rejection of Irish Catholicism,
speaks out with full orchestration:

> Ireland has lain too long under the spell of the magicians,
> without will, without intellect, useless and shameful, the
> despised of nations. I have come into the most impersonal
> country in the world to preach personality – personal love
> and personal religion, personal art, personality for all except
> God; and I walked across the greensward afraid to leave the
> garden, and to heighten my inspiration I looked toward the
> old apple-tree, remembering that many had striven to draw
> forth the sword that Wotan had struck into the tree about
> which Hunding had built his hut. Parnell, like Sigmund, had
> drawn it forth, but Wotan had allowed Hunding to strike
> him with his spear. And the allegory becoming clearer I
> asked myself if I were Siegfried, son of Sigmund slain by
> Hunding, and if it were not my fate to reforge the sword that
> lay broken in halves in Mimi's cave. It seemed to me that the
> garden filled with tremendous music, out of which came a

phrase glittering like a sword suddenly drawn from its sheath and raised defiantly to the sun.[46]

And black and bold on the page the sword motif appears. "Non serviam!" we hear Stephen Dedalus echo, and "Nothung!" as in the smithy of the soul he labours to forge the uncreated conscience of the most belated race in Europe.

"I hear it has to be played on the piano", Oscar Wilde said about some novel of Moore's. As early as the *Confessions of a Young Man* Moore had thought that, just as opera should be endless melody, so the novel should be unbroken narrative[47]; and later, on reading the first novel of "interior monologue" by his friend Dujardin, he saw in it "the daily life of the soul revealed for the first time; a kind of symphony in full stops and commas"[48] – held together, he might have added if he had been capable of observing it at the time, by recurring phrases employed as motifs.

Unlike Joyce, Moore never followed Dujardin in a rigorous "stream of consciousness" technique. To be sure, the story, "Mildred Lawson", opens with a sort of free reverie before moving into the point-of-view technique. Mildred is a low-pulsed Emma Bovary, a more truly ladylike Gerty McDowell. But Moore has no real interest in imitating the process of thought; and the experience of the characters of whom he writes may be disconnected and exterior so long as the melody of his narrative is unbroken. All his later works of fiction are exercises in this one effect, which he believed to be the effect of Wagnerian music drama. He speaks of listening to music and

thinking how a story might be woven from start to finish out of one set of ideas, each chapter rising out of the preceding

[46] *Hail and Farewell, Vale,* London (Heinemann) 1947 (final version) p. 209. The importance of this passage as the culminating statement of a leading theme in the trilogy is pointed out by Wayne Shumaker, *English Autobiography,* Berkeley (University of California Press) 1954, p. 207 and by Herbert Howarth, *The Irish Writers,* London (Rockliff) 1958, pp. 67-8.

[47] *Confessions of a Young Man,* 2nd edn., 1888, pp. 270-1, quoted above, and note 22.

[48] *Letters to Dujardin,* p. 20. See also C. D. King, "Edouard Dujardin, Inner Monologue and the Stream of Consciousness", *French Studies,* VII (1953), pp. 116-28; and Ruth Zabriskie Temple, *The Critic's Alchemy,* New York (Twayne Publishers) 1953, p. 232.

chapter in suspended cadence always, never a full close; and
as an example of the kind of book that comes out of such
ideas as these, I will name "The Brook Kerith," for the story
begins like a brook; the old woman telling stories to her
grandchild may be compared to the "Fanfare of the Rhine,"
and the brook widens out as it flows, a smooth current, not
very rapid, but flowing always, turning sometimes east,
sometimes west, winding, disappearing at last mysteriously
like a river.[49]

The analogy of Moore's late style with Wagner deserves critical
analysis.[50] *Peronnik the Fool* will be appropriate here. It is concise;
it is a treatment of the Parsifal legend, Moore's last return to
Wagnerian theme. The story of Peronnik (the name itself is one
of the many variants of Parsifal) is presented as if recalled and
written down by Héloïse in her convent library. The method of
narration, insinuating, rapid, and without seam, is early established, as in this paragraph:

Her pen kept pace with her memories of Peronnik – how he
had wandered out of the forest and had forgotten everything
except the forest, whither it was still his wont to return
(compelled, maybe, by some homesickness), sometimes
staying away for three or four days, setting the folk talking,
asking each other if they had lost their Peronnik for ever.
She had heard that he once stayed away so long that the folk
had gone forth to seek him, getting tidings of him as they
passed through the fringes of the forest. He passed us by at
daybreak, singing like a lark in the morning, the woodmen

---

[49] "The Nineness in the Oneness", *Century Magazine*, LXXVII (1919),
pp. 65-6. Héloïse, reading Ovid's *Metamorphoses*, "fell to admiring the
strenuous narrative flowing on without a break", *Héloïse and Abélard*, London
(Heinemann) 1952 (reprint of final, 1925, version) pp. 321-2.

[50] Humbert Wolfe finds Moore "anticipating not only Proust but James
Joyce", but "can't understand how he could ever have been captured by
Wagner". *George Moore*, London (Eyre & Spottiswoode) 1931, pp. 1, 37.
Charles Morgan's *Epitaph on George Moore*, New York (Macmillan) 1935,
pp. 52-3, analyses the style without reference to Wagner. Malcolm Brown, in
George Moore: A Reconsideration (p. 182), considers the "problem of adapting
Wagner's form to narrative" and observes Moore's use of "echoes, trans-
formations, modulations, never a full close, always a suspended cadence".

cried; and these tidings were enough for the searchers, who turned back, saying, We shall find him begging his breakfast from somebody, and from us he'll get the thrashing he deserves for having put us to such pains. Why, there he is! cried one, in the doorway of Farmer Leroux's house. Where-upon they stood waiting, fidgeting at their sticks, whilst Peronnik enjoyed such cheer as he could get out of a wooden bowl that all the spoons of the house had already been over. As he scraped and picked the clotted meat from the sides he talked so pleasantly, flattering the good wife so well that she bethought herself of some crusts in her cupboard and returned with her hands full, throwing them one by one into the bowl, for which Peronnik was thankful, gobbling them up with such good appetite that a knight in armour riding by could not do else than rein in his horse to watch him.[51]

It is an individual style, and, sustained throughout an entire book, it does give an impression of continuity if not identical with, at least analogous to Wagner. But what in Wagner is un-broken is the flow of feeling, the never-ending, never-succeeding, never-despairing effort of the orchestra to become articulate or to render articulation superfluous. Moore has no "orchestra" – no feminine, passionate, unconscious line running parallel to the masculine, intellectual, and conscious, nothing of what Yeats calls "emotion of multitude"; and so the analogy is not perfect between unbroken narrative and endless melody. What he does attempt to do, like Mallarmé, is to recapture for literature alone certain qualities of art realised for the first time by Wagner in terms of his composite art; specifically, he attempts to fuse dialogue, descrip-tion, and narrative as Wagner had fused aria, recitative, and orchestra, in the interest of a unified effect. In Moore this effect is curiously level, quiet and monochromatic. This may be so be-cause he was an old man by the time he arrived at his late style. It may also be so because the word cannot (at least in narrative prose – dramatic poetry is another matter) carry the flow of passion as well as the word and music together, as Wagner argued; and, when the word is denied the effects of abruptness and surprise, of discontinuity, one of its chief resources of "musi-

[51] *Peronnik the Fool*, London (Harrap) 1933, p. 6.

cal" appeal is dissipated. The subservience of Debussy to the word led to a similar monotony in *Pélleas et Mélisande*.

Moore's first passion was for painting, his second for literature, his third for music. When Edward Martyn introduced him to Wagner – the sound and presence, not just the literary idea –

> the fanfare of the Rhine told me something undreamed of had come into my life, and I listened as a child listens, understanding nothing, for my poor ears could not follow the intricate weaving and interweaving; my reason tottered like one in a virgin forest, for there seemed to be no path to even a partial understanding of this fulgurent orchestra, predicting at every moment wars and rumours of wars, giants against gods.[52]

Deep as the experience was, it had come too late to penetrate fully into Moore's literary imagination, and only very seldom do we have Wagnerian strong effects. But that is not to discount the importance of the countless small allusions to Wagner and Wagnerian themes and the lifelong effort to obtain in narrative the equivalent of endless melody. "It cannot but be interesting to hear a man tell the story of a great delight, how it came into his life suddenly, and lasted for many years, becoming, without his being aware of the change, a memory sad and sweet, the *lachrymae rerum* of Virgil. The sight of a piano must cause Paderewski to sigh inwardly, and the word Bayreuth comes upon me now like the scent of lavender from an old chest."[53]

[52] "The Nineness in the Oneness", p. 65.
[53] *Op. cit.*, pp. 64-5.

Herbert Howarth

DUBLIN 1899-1911:
THE ENTHUSIASMS OF A
PRODIGAL

In the full spate of a vindictive commentary[1] on his old rival, written years after their quarrels, Yeats paused to admit that five novels by George Moore were an enduring contribution to literature. *Hail and Farewell* did not appear on the list. The book had caricatured Yeats as a middle-class *parvenu*, and the wound still rankled. But *Hail and Farewell* is a masterpiece. Nothing else in English is quite like this trilogy. My purpose here is to survey the days and works that laid a causeway to it, and to notice some of the tasks it performs.

An intricate arrangement of mirrors, in which Moore's private nature and problems, his country's nature and problems, are observed and compared, it is the culmination of twelve years' activity as a wild goose come home. In London of the late 'nineties Moore had taken occasional interest in news of the literary movement and the myths eddying about Irish nationalism. When Yeats and Martyn began rehearsals for their 1899 Irish Drama Festival, they asked him to give them the benefit of his experience of the stage. He agreed; plunged into the literary movement; worked at Irish themes first in the manner of Martyn, then of Yeats; imagined himself the leader or New Man the country was awaiting; took up residence in Dublin; drew attention to himself by gestures which outraged rather than gratified public opinion; dropped the ideology of the literary movement; found his own method of treating Irish themes; developed it; determined that if he could not be a hero, he could be a martyr,

[1] W. B. Yeats, *Dramatis Personae*, New York (Macmillan) 1936, pp. 58-60.

a martyr-satirist, author of the "Sacred Book"[2] without which
political nationalism could not succeed; and in *Hail and Farewell*
fulfilled, by beautifully unexpected twists, the requirements of his
psyche and the potentialities of his art. The last four years of his
Dublin life were spent in the drafting of the trilogy. When the
first volume was ready for publication, he withdrew, like the
protagonist of his "Wild Goose"[3] renewing a voluntary exile.
The whole sequence demonstrates his pattern of assent and
breaking-off, enthusiasm and recoil: his lifelong process of self-
education.

Joining Yeats and Martyn as a director of the Irish Literary
Theatre, Moore took it for granted that his nation expected plays
of him; and unable to see – who could in 1899? – that Ireland
would be in the van of the revolt against naturalism, he decided to
work in the manner and with the materials of Martyn, like himself
a passionate Ibsenist. He relieved Martyn of the script of *The Tale
of a Town* and – calling on Yeats to guide him in the maze of Irish
politics – kneaded it into *The Bending of the Bough*. The play has
seldom been praised, seldom described, yet, like everything that
Moore attempted, it unfolds and refolds at least adequately, and
occasional strokes awaken respect.

The tendency of the Dublin drama movement in its first years
was, alike in its prose and its verse plays, allegorical. *The Bending
of the Bough* is transparent allegory. It purports, with some
passable mimicry, to be a tale of municipal politics. But the
municipality of Northhaven, a byword for poverty, is clearly
Ireland, and the municipality of Southhaven, rich at its neighbour's expense, is clearly England and its Mayor, Mr Hardman,
Lord Salisbury. A few fulgent phrases in Yeats' *Dramatis
Personae*[4] sketch its background: on the report of a Royal Commission that England had overtaxed Ireland by three hundred
million pounds in fifty years, the Protestant landlords, hitherto
the champions of the Union, had revolted, but Lord Salisbury had
bought them off by appointing a second Commission to enquire
into the wrongs of their class. The play shows Southhaven
resisting Northhaven's lawful claims by bribery and chicanery.

---

[2] *Salve*, London (Heinemann) 1947, p. 259.
[3] The penultimate story of *The Untilled Field*, Philadelphia (Lippincott)
1903.   [4] *Dramatis Personae*, pp. 38-9.

Northhaven is the less able to deal with the adroit enemy because her representatives can never agree. Every alderman grinds his own axe, wants to lead or prevent the other leading. But if only a real leader would come . . . ! Here Moore draws the Parnell myth[5] across the allegory. His Jasper Dean is the New Man, the mob-torn Parnell's Messianic successor, of whom Ireland was talking. Dean comes to the municipal struggle sponsored by Alderman Kirwan, a literary idealist, and supported by "the hillside men", the peasants whose allegiance had once strengthened Parnell. With this combination he rallies the Council to the first solid vote it has ever recorded, and the first steps are taken to recover the debt from the great neighbour. Now comes South-haven's counter-attack. It is clever and forcible, but will be defeated if Dean holds firm. His weak point is Hardman's daughter. He sees the danger, decides for the cause instead of for her: but not for long; he has a craving for domesticity; gives up the fight. Northhaven will recede into bickering and servitude till another man appears.

As long as Dean is rallying the community, Moore writes his speeches by borrowing from himself: borrowing his own convert passion for the post-Parnell ideology; borrowing his own hopes that he may become an Irish leader, and his not unreasonable doubts. From Yeats he borrows and puts in the mouth of Kirwan an argument to quench the doubts: "Your appeal is the stronger because you are not of the people; you are the romantic element outside them, the delight they follow always."[6] A landlord like Parnell, and like Parnell distant and romantic by the life he had carved for himself in Paris and London, Moore thought he might be the very stuff for the New Man.

Dean's fatal flaw is not precisely woman but the hearth. As this is gradually exposed, Moore, who let women leave him rather than beguile him into marriage or child-getting, makes an act of detachment, ceases to lend himself to Dean. Yet in the *dénouement*

---

[5] See Herbert Howarth, *The Irish Writers, 1880-1940: Literature under Parnell's Star*, London (Rockliff) 1958.

[6] *The Bending of the Bough*, London (Unwin) 1900, p. 57. This sentence may be contributed by Yeats. The idea sounds like his, so do the words, so does their order. *Cf. Dramatis Personae*, p. 48 (where "Deane" is probably a slip of the pen or the memory for "Kirwan").

there may be, unperceived by him as he wrote it, a foreshadowing of 1911: was not the woman for whom Dean broke away from Northhaven the inner principle, the ultimate psychic loyalty, for which Moore would give up the more obvious loyalties of an Irish nationalist?

The myth of the Irish literary renaissance is represented briefly, but as purely as it will anywhere be found, in the dialogues between Kirwan and Dean. Kirwan is modelled on Standish O'Grady. He cannot himself lead Ireland, but must recognise, announce, and guide the leader. There will be several candidates of adequate capacity. But the moment will be right for only one of them. "If the moment has arrived, you will suffice", Kirwan tells Dean:

> Your speech which carried the Corporation with you and your speeches to the people do not convince me so much of your individual capacity as that the moment has come, and that you really are part and parcel of the movement of a nation.[7]

Kirwan is not infallible; he may mistake the man or the moment. Then he must go back to his vigil, and try again. "The moment"[8] is an echo of Matthew Arnold. In *Hail and Farewell* Moore repeats it and lets us observe how it ran in his mind in 1899.

A minor character of curious interest is Macnee. At first encounter he is one of those servants whom the conventional dramatists drag in for the exposition. But he turns out to embody the Irish "lower depths". Years ago driven out of politics and kept down, but aware of Ireland's necessities and waiting to support the Godot, the Lefty, the new Parnell when man and moment coalesce, he is a figure of political folklore. It is astonishing that Moore or Martyn, landlords, got hold of him. There is a comparable flash of intuition when Dean fails to push the fight against Southhaven. The hillside men, who came into town worshipping their leader and ready to die in his battle, now erupt in fury against their municipality. A collective passion, Moore sees and says, doesn't just disperse when it is thwarted. It explodes among those who should have used it.

---

[7] *The Bending of the Bough*, p. 60.
[8] *Op. cit.*, pp. 59-60. *Cf. Ave*, London (Heinemann) 1947, pp. 28, 116.

Despite its occasional strokes, *The Bending of the Bough*
annoyed Yeats. He disliked its West End business of floor-
scrubbing and tea-drinking. He saw how Moore's eulogies of the
Irish earth fell below poetry. He hated Moore's methods,[9] was
confirmed in his resolution that the naturalistic play should not
capture the Dublin theatre, and moved a little more quickly
towards his discovery of the drama of awe, its figures oversize
silhouettes, their pace on the stage slow, their speech highly-
charged. He moved, by way of Russian opera and ballet and the
Japanese Noh, from allegory to symbol.

Moore himself had an impetuous reaction from *The Bending of
the Bough* to a drama of Irish legend. Conversations with Yeats
and A.E. excited him to a passion for the fancy dress of the Fianna
and (to do justice to the clever man under the pseudo-simpleton)
for the prospect of eliciting elemental truths of human behaviour
from Celtic saga as Wagner had elicited them from German. He
and Yeats undertook a play of Diarmuid and Grania. They tus-
sled stubbornly with one another; tried to allay their difficulties
by apportioning[10] the responsibilities: Yeats yielded to Moore
the last word on the construction, Moore yielded to Yeats the last
word on the language. The three-act work was performed by
Frank Benson's English company in Dublin in the autumn of
1901. It is habitually described as a failure. Moore, glad to claim
that he shocked local puritanism, says that an outcry[11] arose when
Grania was found short of Irish chastity. Yeats, however,
remembers that the applauding crowd[12] surrounded his cab after
the performance and offered to remove the horse from the shafts
and drag him (and Maud Gonne) in triumph. What is certain is
that the English production that was expected to follow the
Dublin première never followed, and the two men never published
their text. Their growing jealousy of one another, both of them
"violent, discordant"[13] men, is probably the reason for their

[9] See W. B. Yeats, *Letters*, ed. Allan Wade, London (Hart-Davis) 1954,
pp. 440-1, for a marvellous display of Yeats working towards his future
position as he coaches Frank Fay to resist Moore's naturalism.

[10] Yeats, *op. cit.*, p. 347.

[11] Joseph Hone, *George Moore*, New York (Macmillan) 1936, p. 239. *Cf.*
Martyn's rather different disapproval, *Salve*, p. 92.

[12] Joseph Hone, *W. B. Yeats*, New York (Macmillan) 1943, p. 181.

[13] So Yeats calls Moore in *Dramatis Personae*, p. 60.

neglect to publish. William Becker, the editor to whom goes the credit of at last examining a typescript and getting it into print in the *Dublin Magazine* (April-June, 1951), preferred[14] the familiar reason, "neither Yeats nor Moore thought the play worthy of publication". But the Grania story is so powerful that if a mind of any sensibility handles it, something must come through; and even two mutually-repellent sensibilities brought something through.

A wedding is to unite the Fianna, Ireland's fighting clan, with her king, and thus to ensure the expulsion of her enemies. The bridegroom, Finn, chief of the Fianna, is past his youth. At the wedding-feast Grania drugs the guests, all but three young men, with the best of whom, Diarmuid, she takes flight to the woods. Devoted to Finn, Diarmuid swears never to possess her. Eventually she prevails on him. For seven years they are hunted by the chief. Foreign enemies fall on disrupted Ireland, and do such havoc that the feud is patched up in a fresh bid for unity. Finn and Diarmuid swear a blood-bond. But Diarmuid senses that Grania now desires the elder man. It is agreed that both men shall hunt the wild boar and Grania be the prize of the successful hunter. Diarmuid is killed by the wild beast. The play ends with the crow of a cynic[15]: "Grania makes great mourning for Diarmuid, but her welcome to Finn shall be greater."

Deirdre, whose love-death bears an obvious analogy to Isolde's, has been adopted as the world's Irish heroine, and today there is one man who knows Grania's story for a hundred who know Deirdre's. But Grania's is the more energetic. Easy to see how it engaged the fancy of a Moore who had the grace to be woman-mad. By what methods, and after how many attempts, did she subdue Diarmuid's loyalty? Moore delighted in the folk-report of her temptings: when they had to cross a stream[16] and her legs were wetted, she said, "Diarmuid, you are a great warrior, but the

---

[14] In *The Variorum Edition of the Plays of W. B. Yeats*, ed. R. K. Alspach, New York (Macmillan) 1966, p. 1169. This edition reprints *The Dublin Magazine* text of *Diarmuid and Grania* and William Becker's useful introductory note.

[15] *Op. cit.*, p. 1222.

[16] *The Untilled Field*, p. 277. Lady Gregory later reports much the same saying in the notes to her *Grania* in *Irish Folk History Plays*: but she takes the edge off it.

water is braver than you!" There was no room for the wading
scene in the play and he had to let that go, though he saved it for
The Untilled Field. In substitution he invented a parallel, less
lively but not lifeless: "Mais, Diarmuid, la pomme qui est tombée
dans ma robe . . . regarde-la: elle ose plus que toi."[17] That in
turn was evicted from the play, perhaps by Yeats, who was still
proper, not yet ready for the somersault of the 'twenties. Enough
remained of Grania's fierce brooding on Diarmuid, her first direct
demand on him, to gratify the sexual psychologist in Moore.
And why after seven years did she grow tired of life with Diarmuid in their rich valley, brood on Finn whom she had once
rejected, and turn and seduce the old fighter? That question
stimulated Moore to two pages that give actress and actor some
opportunity to disturb the theatre.

An open-air lushness abounds in the play. On his return to
Ireland Moore was roused to recollection of his boyhood pleasure
in wood and lake. There are passages of springing sap in all his
Irish books. In 1900 the pleasure ran free, as yet almost uncom-
mented and uncorrected by thought. The naturalist in Yeats
cooperated to give *Diarmuid and Grania* stand after stand of wild
life imagery: "birds beasts and leaves which ever way I turned"[18];
fat cattle in the valleys; otter and salmon in the streams. Early
Ireland, says Moore in another book, was a Land of Woods.[19]
There is savagery too: the wolves, the acorn-fed boars. It is hard
to know, the drama hints, whether a natural ferocity or a natural
fruitfulness will grow fastest in Ireland, whether the land will
prosper or be torn apart by its own primitive violence as much as
by the invader.

In later years the Yeats of the mature, highly-compressed plays
observed that Moore's much-vaunted "construction" let redund-
ancies into *Grania*. Strictly speaking, it did. Moore wrote a piece
of sheep-shearing "business" to open, and to defer, the second
act. Yeats, equally, was responsible for a piece of "business" in
the first act, the hanging of the shields of the Fianna.[20] Both
these digressions are in fact attractive; both point their authors to

[17] *Ave*, p. 277.
[18] Alspach's edition, p. 1198.
[19] *Ave*, p. 263: "The Island of Many Woods".
[20] See Becker in Alspach's edition, pp. 1170-1.

the future. Moore was enraptured by the sheep-shearing and
theorised how "Man has shorn sheep since the beginning and the
wars and the strife will break in upon Arcady as they always have
done".[21] Over the next fifteen years it became his policy to work
for strokes which took his audience or his readers back to the
foundation experiences of culture. The sheep wriggling under
Benson's arm became the sheep which Christ tends in *The Brook
Kerith*. Yeats felt his way from the pageantry of the shields to
dream-giants and heraldry. Durrell's "heraldic universe" inter-
rupts in that first act of 1901. And at the centre of *Diarmuid and
Grania* the ritual of the blood-bond – Diarmuid and Finn slash
themselves, drip blood into a goblet and drink it, while an in-
cantation, the only verse of the play, is sung – is a saga version of
the ritual that Eliot was to place at the centre of *The Cocktail Party*
nearly half-a-century later, since which date the modern theatre
at large has been ritual-bound.

With a characteristic shift Moore shied away from heroic drama
as fast as he had rushed into it. He had speared permanent
acquisitions from the Celtic cauldron for his later works. But his
tendency was to quotidianise the heroes. He wanted not Yeats'
dream world but the real world which Yeats affected to despise.
In *Ave* he recalls Yeats debating the construction of *The Shadowy
Waters*: ". . . my thoughts wandered from the Fomorians to the
autumn landscape, full of wonderful silence and colour, and I
begged Yeats to admire with me the still lake filled with the broad
shadow of the hill . . . and it seemed to me that we could do
nothing better than watch the landscape fixed in the lake as in a
mirror. But Yeats' mind was whirling with Fomorians. . . ."[22]
The nationalist passion for ancient Ireland, says the satire, stood
between the Irish and reality.

For the first two years Moore lacked the right form to bring
his gifts for the visible and tangible to bear on Ireland's affairs.
He found a form in the short story. Almost every writer cares for
the regeneration of language, and he had imposed his support on
the Gaelic League. Students[23] of the revived Gaelic, he reflected
one day, must find their manuals slow going. "Put the butter on

[21] *Loc. cit.* Becker's and Alspach's text shows that Moore wrote "strive".
[22] *Ave*, p. 187. *Cf.* p. 192.
[23] *Salve*, pp. 108-9.

the floor"[24] was sub-ecstatic. Give them stories from *The Arabian Nights* and they would press on. *Not* the *Nights*! retorted the chastity-conscious League. Eglinton suggested Turgenev as a better model, Moore glimpsed what might be done, and Father Finlay offered to print in *The New Ireland Review* tales to carry the readers forward without detriment to their spiritual welfare.

Moore began with "The Wedding Gown" which answered the specifications, a tale as perfect as Lawrence's "Rocking-Horse Winner". Lawrence studies the misunderstanding in our time of the spark of luck; Moore's is a timeless study of the spark of happiness. We cling to a momentary happiness in a symbol, till we meet someone, a self reborn, to whom it can be passed on, and then we are free to die. "The Wedding Gown" has nothing to do with Ireland; as a matter of fact it reached Moore from Lancashire; essentially it is placeless as well as timeless. Then he wrote "The Clerk's Quest" and "Alms-Giving", sentimental and philanthropic, suitable for Father Finlay, rather meagre as stories. Warmed up by these essays, he felt his gifts come alive, reached his subject: real Ireland, as she looked to the native returned, his eye taught by other scenes to see her with the clarity of contrast, his memory teaching him to plot her history over the forty years since his childhood. He made such progress that "Home Sickness" and "Exile" terminated his collaboration with *The New Ireland Review* and the plan for a student *Reader*. That freed him. He now advanced to the time-full, point-making stories that showed the barren places in the Irish lushness, decay driving out vitality. "Story followed story, each coming into my mind before the story on the blotting-pad was finished, and each suggested by something seen or something heard." And "Each story . . . helped me to understand my own country".[25] A certain kind of writer may know what he has to write not before but only in the act of writing, as *The Untilled Field* testifies.

Two moods intersect in *The Untilled Field*: sympathy with what is generous, naive, and brave in the Irish; a protest against the forces that enfeeble and depopulate Ireland. Moore's closing story tells how the pathos of the landscape and the wistfulness of the people call to him. His literary rivals took these appeals for

[24] Susan Mitchell, *George Moore*, New York (Dodd, Mead) 1916, gives the example.   [25] *Salve*, pp. 123-5.

granted, thought them poor in heroic admonishment, left them unexpressed. It is wrong to withhold our sympathy from any side of life, Moore once said,[26] praising himself a little; but it is true that beneath his grimacing masks of the landlord and the bohemian lay inexhaustible sympathy; and he gave it scope. He created Father MacTurnan, who has chosen the poorest district in Ireland for his parish, who labours for its relief, who courageously pursues quixotic fantasies: builds a playhouse in the waste for the performance of Mysteries; petitions Rome to abrogate the rule of celibacy so that the clergy, the only Irish with the income to raise children, may replenish the nation. "A Letter to Rome" is a village comedy of sweetness and light. The brother priest who advises Father MacTurnan not to mail his letter, the Archbishop who examines him, are drawn as humanely as the petitioner. Never have the clergy been so considerately, even lovingly, caricatured. Side by side with these charities, however, Moore poises his criticisms. Some of the parish priests are puritans, scolds, bullies. They kill the courting and dancing. No one can stand up to the fulminations of a priest: but the young, or the strongest of them, leave the country. The emigration that is impoverishing Ireland of talent is hastened by clerical despotism. Moore dramatises his charges in scenes not overloaded, sentences not overpitched. Only once or twice he releases a bolt . . . the prettiest girl in Father MacTurnan's parish, who was to play Good Deeds[27] in the Mystery, was "wake" one evening on the road home from rehearsal, "and when the signs of her weakness began to show upon her, her mother took the halter off the cow and tied the girl to the wall and kept her there until the child was born. And Mrs Sheridan put a piece of string round its throat and buried it one night near the playhouse".

So, having returned to Ireland as a sympathiser, Moore has arrived at the point where he is equally sympathiser and critic. His next step goes deeper into criticism. Watching his own movements, since he finds himself the most interesting character any artist invented, he notices that he has become a protester. He promptly revises the word to fit his clerical theme: he is a Pro-

---

[26] *The Lake*, N.Y. (Appleton) 1929, p. 232. This edition is identical with the final revision (Heinemann) 1921.

[27] *The Untilled Field*, p. 217.

testant. Now he has a thesis. If every Irish Catholic would renounce docility and become strenuously Protestant, what a
stirring! Ireland would get her freedom, the countryside its
rehabilitation, the national genius its arts. He spent a year
revolving the theme and debating it with his friends, and in the
autumn of 1903 took the notorious step[28] described in *Hail and
Farewell*: publicly declared himself a Protestant and said that
Ireland's independence could only be achieved when Irishmen
asserted their intellect and personality without the regulation of
the ancient Church.

The inner debate which culminated in these public histrionics
underlies his next book, *The Lake*. It is the chronicle of a priest,
as devoted and hardworking as the best men in *The Untilled Field*.
Horrified to learn that the village schoolteacher is pregnant,
Father Gogarty denounces unchastity from his pulpit, then
gradually discovers that his sermon was prompted by jealousy
and craving. What begins as a battle to keep Rose a good
Catholic, lest his soul be burned for driving her from Ireland into
a dangerous world, becomes an appreciation of his "crushed
instincts",[29] which revive and define themselves, till he knows
that he must abandon both the satisfaction of his daily labour for
his flock and the ease of his village house for the satisfaction of
the daily fight for life in the hurly-burly of lay America. *The
Untilled Field* had begun as a gift to the Gaelic League, which
combated emigration. Its sequel *The Lake*, is the justification of
an *émigré*.

But in *The Lake* the inner debate, which is in reality seething,
tumultuous, not to say muddled, as we know from *Hail and
Farewell*, where it is Moore's purpose to betray his mixed motives,
is subdued to a clear quiet, overlaid by a summer haze. The tone
is an extraordinary demonstration of his restraint, his ability to
smooth away ripples and crinkles. He seems to endow his
rejection of the Church with the virtues of patience and solicitude.
The object of the book is to beckon the man out of the priest, yet
he makes us care for the priest in the man: the parish priest who
must be "scrivener, land valuer, surveyor, and engineer",[30] who
gives a new suit to ragged Pat Kearney, who walks his drinking

[28] It provides the climax of *Salve*. *Cf.* Hone, *George Moore*, pp. 249-51.
[29] *The Lake*, p. 254.   [30] *Op. cit.*, p. 297.

curate, Father Moran, through a crisis. There is full play of the
sympathy that gentled *The Untilled Field*. In certain episodes the
reader can hardly say what it is that moves him: in the talk
between Gogarty and his sister,[31] the practical Superioress of a
Convent, for example: the dialogue is commonplace, but Moore
makes the understanding between brother and sister flow through
the spaces between the words. "That artless man",[32] Yeats called
Moore. But the low voice is art.

Like Gide's *Immoraliste* of three years earlier, *The Lake* is an
exercise in double counterpoint. In the first half of the narrative
the priest instructs Rose, towards the end she lends her wisdom
to him. She, an expression of the instincts, symbolised in the
carnation, moves to a quickening cerebral life; he, who was the
cleverest man of his year at Maynooth, learns to forget ideas and
to follow feeling. She goes deep into the east to trace "the
sources of the Christian river"; he turns west to America and
secularism. If in our time this seems too neat, and if the inversions
can now be manipulated by many writers, it was fresh and elating
in 1905. To informal Ireland the form was one of Moore's gifts.

In 1900 his tendency was to ask what the Irish were doing and
to throw himself into their effort with a splash. By 1905 he rather
asked what the Irish were conspicuously omitting to do, and what
he must pour into the national lacuna to make them do it. He
supplied his talent for organisation; his intelligence; his cosmo-
politanism, or what Eglinton calls "a far wider culture than that
with which he was commonly credited".[33] Through the sentimental texture of *The Lake* he draws sinewy threads of ideas. He
works with Barrès' doctrine of the Self: "We must not think
entirely of our duties to others; we must think of our duties to
ourselves. Each one must try to bring these gifts that Nature
gave us to fruition."[34] He works with the comparative religion
to which his friend Dujardin has alerted him: by a short, sound
explanation of the discipline he invites Ireland to notice that
Catholicism is only a phase of the Christian story, Christianity only
a phase in a larger religious evolution. *Hail and Farewell* flicks

[31] *Op. cit.*, pp. 92-4.
[32] Quoted by Becker in Alspach's edition, p. 1170.
[33] John Eglinton, *A Memoir of A. E.*, London, (Macmillan) 1937, p. 70.
[34] *The Lake*, p. 239.

around mordantly with comparative religion; it is a whip to hurt his friends. In *The Lake* it is applied with sweet reason. It was in fact one of the revelations of Moore's life. It divested the Bible figures forced on him in boyhood of that indisputable authority which provoked his rebellion; it allowed him to approach them with unchecked curiosity. Moore's development from *The Lake* through *Hail and Farewell* to *The Brook Kerith* shows that at the age of fifty a man may still be transformed by a revelation and put it to creative use.

And comparative religion gave a new lease of life to the paganism which he had proclaimed as a poet in 1881 and as an autobiographer in 1888. Although he began to write *The Lake* as a demonstration of his "Protestant" meditations, his rapid thinking swirled as he wrote, and the novel is a salute to his paganism rediscovered. Like the concurrent work of a much younger man, Forster, whom he probably did not know, *The Lake* turns Shelley's and Swinburne's instinctive dancing of Aegean mythology into fables in which a cerebral conviction that "it should be so" blends with a pulse affirmation that "it can be so, it is so": a literature of the years after *The Golden Bough*. When people said that their blood had been thinned by puritanism or rationalism and that they needed the sense of the earth and the seasonal rituals, Moore the better understood himself. He had always been trying to live the Pan of whom the others were beginning to talk and write. His inveterate perversity and prurience were Pan-simulations. He now asked Ireland to emulate him. There is a first flash of this lesson in *The Untilled Field*: "When, I said, will a ray from the antique sun break forth and light up this country again?"[35] *The Lake* is an elaboration of the question. Gogarty likens himself, and likens Ireland with whom he is equated throughout the book, to "an old, decrepit house with sagging roof and lichen-covered walls, and all the doors and windows nailed up. Every generation nailed up a door or a window till all were nailed up. . . . About the house the doleful sound of shutters creaking on rusty hinges never ceases."[36] Rose Leicester, the principle of the springtide,[37] comes, and a

[35] *The Untilled Field*, p. 202.
[36] *The Lake*, p. 256.
[37] *Op. cit.*, p. 240.

shutter drops away, "and I found myself looking at the splendid sun".

"God gave us our human nature",[38] pagan Moore preaches to puritan Ireland. He leads Father Gogarty step by step to the realisation that "body and mind . . . are not two things, but one thing",[39] and that the whole man must live integrally. A Father Gogarty who remained a priest, an Ireland that remained obedient to the atrophied Irish branch of Catholicism, would be like the curlew that collapses on the eyot, and is found to be maimed by some accident or cruelty, a wild bird[40] with its legs tied together.

The Lake is a work of polemic. Yet on a modern reader the impression it leaves is of composition: material worked to coherence; a deliberate harmony; a paradigm of the unity of body and mind. In a copy in the University of Pennsylvania Library some reader, some time since 1929, has annotated Chapter XIV, "Not even Turgenev could have written this chapter". Excessive praise, perhaps: but it illustrates how Moore's composing and his subdued persuasion have often gratified.

I may appear to have lost sight of the realist touches and the occasional brutalities in *The Lake*: the cottagers going behind the hedge, the air of the village heavy; the fierce story of the thirteenth-century Barretts offering their prisoners the choice between blinding and castration. The very success of Moore's technique in merging the details of *The Lake* in a delicate haze means that in retrospect we do lose sight of these incidents. When he turned to write *Hail and Farewell* Moore set himself a harder task: in a more complicated design, in which the risk of losing the detail was heightened, to etch every episode so clearly that the memory would not amend it or subdue it.

In *Hail and Farewell* he narrates the story of his Dublin return, describes the literary movement, his enthusiastic attempts to participate, his recoil, and the crystallisation of his dissidence. That is the skeleton of his plan. Its flesh is an intricate explanation, a search for causes. He explores himself, going back to his boyhood and youth to understand the patterns of conduct; and he examines Ireland, anatomising her character, asking what she has been, what she is, where she fails. It is a work of derision and compassion. He knows that he will wound, admits that he *wants*

[38] *Op. cit.*, p. 232.   [39] *Op. cit.*, p. 259.   [40] *Op. cit.*, p. 251.

to wound. He has his secret personal reasons for wounding. But the public reasons for it are good. The Sacred Book of Ireland cannot flatter, must hurt. It is a sacrificial undertaking, because it will be resented in the measure it succeeds. Moore's comic picture of himself as the martyr-prophet has been verified by events; there are Irishmen who still shudder at his name. He struck with all his force; he put everything he knew into the writing.

The great nineteenth-century example of a Sacred Book, a myth of the national character in which a people saw itself, was Wagner's *Ring*, which Moore remembers and discusses throughout *Hail and Farewell*. *The Ring* determines the scale of his work: *The Ring* a tetralogy, *Hail and Farewell* a trilogy. *The Ring* determines his plan of dispersal and re-iteration: he sets himself several "topics", disputes them not each in one place but at intervals across his three volumes, reverting to them and developing them; and he expects a frequent reader to follow them as the Wagnerite follows the *motifs*. The difference between Wagner and Moore is that Wagner takes himself with the simplicity of the sublime, believes every word he says and every bar he scores. Moore talks with the flourishes and subterfuges of the comedian, assumes that every man says one thing[41] and believes another, and shows the interplay of pretence and conviction. Critics may urge that *Hail and Farewell* is mock-heroic. In fact, it encompasses a mock-heroic technique, in which Wagner is Moore's panel of reference as Homer is Fielding's or Joyce's: but like *Ulysses* it goes far beyond mock-heroic and its figures are the more heroic for being foolish.

"What do you think I came to Ireland for?"[42] Moore asked A.E., and received the answer: to be an Irish Voltaire: ridicule the bishops; put down the pompous. He ridicules the bishops a little. He ridicules those who accept clerical authority, his brother and cousin for instance, ready to switch off their lively intellects at a hint from the Church. Much more he ridicules the pontiffs of nationalism; the chieftains of the post-Parnell groups; the new Irish bards; even the agricultural organisers struggling with the Augean stables. He ridicules himself. He is the hero of his book,

[41] *Cf. Ave*, p. 77: "In Ireland we don't mean all we say".
[42] *Salve*, p. 118.

but a comic hero,[43] one of the first of the "anti-heroes". Ireland is famous for her sense of comedy. All too famous, thought Moore: her drolleries tend to be as conventional as the commercial stage; and he spent twenty years undervaluing the comic powers which brightened *A Modern Lover* and his *Confessions*. When he heard that Yeats was writing *The Pot of Broth* he cried "Disgraceful!"[44] Then almost at once he came round from his abhorrence, saw the possibilities, summoned his powers, and fully deployed them in *Hail and Farewell*. *Hail and Farewell* is one of the great comic works of the English language. But it is a great medley, comedy only one of its elements. The tones change, and change again, from the nostalgic to the grotesque, from the sentimental to the argumentative and aggressive. This is to do the work that A.E. often urged: to call Ireland's assumptions into doubt; to make her think.

For the object of the ridicule is not quite the classical object, that the victims be "touched and shamed", but that they be liberated.[45] A Sacred Book is to set all Ireland free. But the strategist in Moore saw that it was impracticable to reach all Ireland, and that he must set free – set free by insult – those who had acquired some authority as leaders of Ireland. Change them, and the change might spread downwards. They seemed to be stiffening in strange postures. His book invites them to see themselves, unflex, feel the blood circulate again, think Ireland's problems again in a wider context. Satire alone would not have been sufficient. The need was for gymnastics, for rapid intellectual and emotional shifts. *Hail and Farewell* is versatile to induce versatility.

Yeats was the authority he respected most; against whom, consequently, he organised his liveliest attacks. The procedures of the trilogy were in some measure decided by his resolve to contradict, discomfort, or outbid Yeats. He saw an opening on the issue of "folk", and drove at it with marvellous results. Yeats thought that "folk" is at its best in the tales and songs of the countryside which preserve the life and myths of the remote past. Moore replied that "folk" is at its freshest in the rumour, humour,

---

[43] Since Moore is attacking Irish heroics, which obfuscate the real world, he *must* refuse to be a heroic hero.　　　　　　　　　[44] *Salve*, p. 98.

[45] *Cf. Vale*, London (Heinemann) 1947, p. 257, "a work of liberation".

gossip that spill from current events. "If a story be told three or four times by different people it becomes folk."[46] "We shall all become folklore in time to come, Finns and Diarmuids and Usheens, every one of us, and" (with malice) "Lady Gregory a new Niamh".[47] *Hail and Farewell* is a book of folklore, the activities of the nationalists chronicled as they happened, their words, including their words about and against one another, caught live off their lips. Moore extends the anecdotes into full-length portraits, portraits into family histories, family histories into national history. So, for example, with the eight-hundred-year history of the Martyns. And so with his own family record, for which of course he has the amplest material: through his forerunners and himself he gets at the history and mental make-up of the Irish, those "queer people, the queerest in the world",[48] as he had called them in *The Lake*. The gallery of portraits, of which some critics complained, is a book of the nation. It is a dazzling outcome of the contest with Yeats. Yeats, clever in learning from his rivals, saw the point. Resenting Moore's caricatures, he nevertheless assimilated the method of the Personal Portrait into his lyrics and his prose.

Moore made comparable gains by fighting Yeats and Lady Gregory on the dialect question. In 1899 he was captivated by their experiments with Celtic "idiom". Literary English, he mutters in *Salve*, has "breeze and bite in it", but is "a declining language . . . weary with child-bearing"[49]; and he welcomed the infusion of Irish. Then his neophyte transports burned out, and he manœuvred to outflank Yeats. In *Hail and Farewell* he picks holes in Lady Gregory's Kiltartan,[50] claims that she doesn't know enough about the dialect of her district, and writes his own displays of Irish English to show that he can do it better. More important, he sees, what his more narrowly Irish friends could not see, that any dialect, feelingly used, will invigorate English, and demonstrates it by laying a chapter in Sussex[51] and embodying the down dialect.

A younger Yeats of the 'eighties had walked Ireland and talked to the country people, and the experience had set him working

[46] *Ave*, p. 108.   [47] *Op. cit.*, p. 264.   [48] *The Lake*, p. 74.
[49] *Salve*, p. 127.   [50] *Vale*, pp. 126-31.
[51] *Ave*, pp. 235-50. *Cf. Salve*, p. 202.

towards a language of immediate sensation. *Hail and Farewell*
insinuates two charges. The Yeats of 1900 had lost touch with
the peasants, was now taking his knowledge at second-hand: Lady
Gregory braved the "suffocating interior" of a cottage,[52] while
Yeats gracefully awaited her under the hawthorn. And: Yeats
had always restricted his interest to the poor of the countryside,
whereas Moore had discovered that the poor of the cities as well
as the poor of the countryside spoke the intimate language which
teaches a writer both the truth about the heart and the way to tell
it. Some of the autobiographical material in *Hail and Farewell* is a
claim to the better literary education. In a London garret,[53] he
says, he had listened to the talk of his cleaning-woman, and it had
given him *Esther Waters*. When *Esther* had made him prosperous,
he had moved to more expensive chambers – and had lost his
teacher! But re-settling in Dublin he had come back within
earshot of living speech. The chatter of two washerwomen rose
from the poor cottages behind Ely Place, and he congratulated
himself, "A man of letters never objects to a slum. He sharpens
his pen there."[54] A landlord's patronising way of putting it! But
underneath the drawl there is the idea. And he really responds to
other voices and learns sometimes to abnegate his Establishment
voice and to feel and write with them.

In the total structure of *Hail and Farewell* the commentary on
language and the exhibitions of dialect depend from the "topic"
of *nature versus art*, one of the motif questions debated through the
trilogy. Since Yeats maintained the pre-eminence of art, Moore
found himself obliged to advocate the pre-eminence of nature.
Synge's greatness, he says, and the value of Jack Yeats' painting
come from their indifference to art and their passion for life,[55] and
as for himself anything he has ever done well has been done from
nature. He does not hold this position with absolute consistency,
but he shows extraordinary suppleness in adapting material which
for other reasons, and sometimes entirely for its own sake, he wants
to include in the trilogy, to the reinforcement of his case. It would
be unthinkable for him to omit his reminiscences of the French
Impressionists. So he attaches these to the question of nature-or-
art. With a nicely insidious half-truth he infers that his quick

[52] *Ave*, p. xi.   [53] *Op. cit.*, pp. 67-8.   [54] *Salve*, p. 9.
[55] *Vale*, pp. 140-1. *Cf. Vale*, p. 168 on A.E.

response to Impressionism was involved with his appreciation of
dialect, of the common events of daily life, of the appeal of the
poor. His adolescent sketches, he claims in *Vale*, were shown to
an old-fashioned practitioner of the sublime, James Browne:

> but he did not seem to think much of them, and on my
> pressing my mother to tell me more I dragged the truth from
> her that he considered girls riding bicycles showing a great
> deal of stocking a low form of art.[56]

Under the impudently modest tone this is a bold claim: that he had
fore-felt Impressionism, that his eye had adopted the subjects of
Degas – "shop-girls, ballet-girls, washerwomen"[57] – five or six
years before the first Impressionist Exhibition. At this point and
elsewhere in *Hail and Farewell* he slides towards us items meant in
their total to make us think that both Impressionism and dialect
radiate a quintessential life unshielded by the guards of convention, and that the rediscovery of dialect was to literature what
Impressionism was to painting. By a less devious argument
Moore professes that the comedy of *Hail and Farewell* is not art
but nature. The weirder it seems, the more faithfully it is drawn
from life. Only nature could have invented Martyn. Moore's
excursions around the theme of nature spin the hallucination of
an aesthetic by which the whole conduct of *Hail and Farewell*, the
parade of his own nature, his family's, friends', neighbours', and
his country's, is justified.

There is nothing so shocking to a man as his own face in the
glass, nothing so likely to wrest an effort out of him. In the forefront of Moore's plan is the promise he made himself when Yeats
was absent among the Fomorians: to show his country to his
country. He does it, through those vital, grotesque portraits of
people. And he does it through topography. Between the portraits come the scenes in the image of which Irishmen grow.[58]
The path down the Dodder; the houses of Galway; grey Manulla
Junction and its bridge, sky, and telegraph wires: the shots

[56] *Op. cit.*, p. 21.
[57] *Confessions of a Young Man*, London (Heinemann) 1952 (identical with
1937 edition) p. 29 Chap. 4, describes the Impressionist Exhibition.
[58] *Cf. The Untilled Field*, p. 186, "The land had made them . . . according to
its own image".

appear on the screen of his pages clear, sensuous, and immediate. Max Beerbohm told Virginia Woolf that Moore never used his eyes, merely pillaged books, but at her demurrer conceded, "Ah I was afraid you would remind me of *Ave atque Vale*. Yes, that's beautiful. Yes, it's true he used his eyes there."[59]

In fact, he shows two Irelands. He had thought, when he planned the book, how he would document with nostalgic pleasure what he knew intimately, the Ireland of his boyhood: landlords and tenantry at Communion in Carnacun Chapel; the butcher killing pigs by the dung-heap; the harriers on a bleak hillside; "Joe Blake going off to Castlebar races with his arms round his serving-maid's waist"[60]; "the tarts on Kingstown Pier on Sundays beautifully dressed in sea-green dresses and sealskin jackets".[61] He had detected a danger: a book of memories might seem as light as the old Irish novels of Lever and Lover.[62] The removal of this danger was among the several advantages he won as he elaborated and convoluted the design of his trilogy. By the difficult and elegant system of the double autobiography,[63] which narrates his experiences of forty years back while narrating the experiences of middle age, he shows two Irelands, and the feat raises him from the raconteur to the social historian. He is the annalist of the death of the landlords. Some of the early episodes of *Ave* are memories of Moore Hall in its heyday, abrim with the vitality of a spending squire. At the end of *Vale* Moore travels to the estate for a last visit, sees the dilapidation, foresees the Götterdämmerung:

> We are a disappearing class, our lands are being confiscated, and our houses are decaying or being pulled down to build cottages for the folk. All that was has gone or is going. . . . In another fifty years Ireland will have lost all the civilisation

[59] Virginia Woolf, *A Writer's Diary*, London (Hogarth Press) 1953, p. 306. Contrast *Salve*, p. 4: "only what my eye has seen, and my heart has felt, interests me".

[60] *Vale*, p. 212 (taking up the master and servant-mistress motif from *Ave*).

[61] *Salve*, p. 89.

[62] *Ave*, pp. 4, 25.

[63] Again and again Moore executes a subordinate double-play within this over-all scheme: *e.g. Salve*, pp. 224-7, a conversation which purports to show how no two people remember the same things, but shows the school, the schoolboy Moore, and his father clear through the refractory medium.

of the eighteenth century and will be a swamp of peasants with a priest here and there. . . .[64]

This is not a blind nostalgia. He has pointed out that feudalism continued in Ireland till 1870. He has reported, with pungency, the beastliness that went with the graces of the *ancien régime*. He has shown (what none of his English contemporaries who sang neo-feudalism seemed to know) that a landlord cared less about the tenants than the cattle. He could remember resting his horse in a peasant's one-room cabin: and the evictions, the holdings turned over to grass. There *is* something of every ageing man's regret at change because it obliterates his world: but he would forego the regret if he could see a lively new world appearing in its place. He sees none. Only the encroachment of ruin and weed. The renaissance that might have re-civilised Ireland will not come.

It is obvious today where Moore fell short. As the descriptive observer of certain segments of his people, the landlords, tenantry, and clergy of the countryside, the intelligentsia of Dublin, he is unsurpassed. But he was poor in prognosis. He did not guess, when he reiterated the motif that Irish dreams and reality are widely separated, that dreams sometimes transform reality. He did not guess how the myth-figures, the "mysterious kinsmen"[65] of O'Grady, Yeats, and A.E., would evoke a latent strength of the people, energise the young to turn the national dream of independence into reality.

But accurate prognosis was not his intention. His intention was to irritate the "creatures of marsh and jungle",[66] to get Ireland moving out of her sloth, almost regardless of the direction she might choose when she moved. He told her she was beyond help. It was a way of helping.

Beneath the national intention Moore had two deeper intentions; and it is a peculiar beauty of *Hail and Farewell* that it displays the symptoms of them and wills – "intends" – that they be identified. The first was to write a book such as no one had conceived before. He would, he avows, do anything for a book.

[64] *Vale*, p. 245.
[65] A.E., "On an Irish Hill", in *Imaginations and Reveries*, Dublin (Maunsel) 1915.   [66] *Salve*, p. 100.

He does. He tells the tale of his impotence; brings the obloquy of a nation about his ears; propels himself over the curve, from the fringe in to the centre, from the centre out to Golgotha, of the Messiahs, all of whom fall "punctured"[67] – a recurring, ludicrous image of the trilogy. The result *is* an unprecedented book. It pioneers, among other things, that self-conscious twentieth-century form, the Making of the Made: the form that observes itself *en train de se faire*. The second intention was to defy his family. Dispersing the evidence over the three volumes, he explains how his father, whose verve and audacity he loved, regarded him as "a stupid little boy",[68] how his mother[69] disbelieved in him. He grew to expect ridicule; and he developed an instinct of "rebellion against all authority".[70] When he came to Dublin in 1899 he carried an English reputation home with him; another man might have been acclaimed: but the Irish met his underground doubts of himself half-way, and soon he was working furiously for a repetition of the pattern of his life, doing all he could to bring rejection on himself, doing all he could to turn the rejection to triumph by the brilliance of his retaliation. *Hail and Farewell* is the crown of the process. The title is associated with the last pieties at the grave of a brother; Moore returned to Ireland and committed every impiety on his brother. He burned his family in the effigy of Colonel Maurice Moore, of his cousin Edward Martyn, and of Ireland herself. But there came to him the positivism which comes to an artist in the act of destruction, as if the immense outburst has broken his cage and enlarged him; and in the book which harries and hurts his family and country, he writes a delighted, dashing impression of his father and performs the therapy of art for Ireland.

[67] *Cf. Ave*, pp. 109, 110, 126; *Salve*, pp. 43, 48.
[68] *Ave*, pp. 61-2.   [69] *E.g. Ave*, p. 199.   [70] *Ave*, p. 182.

Graham Owens

THE MELODIC LINE IN NARRATIVE

Moore had returned to Ireland at the end of the century in order to "recreate" himself once more, and it was in the Ireland of Yeats that he discovered the style which was the foundation of all his later work. True, the germ of this style is to be found earlier: Malcolm Brown[1] locates the beginnings in *Parnell and his Island*.[2] Moreover, Moore's cast of mind had been shaped by a variety of influences. Flaubert and Gautier, Turgenev and Jane Austen, Landor and Pater – all had left their mark. And Moore himself loved to romanticise the sources of his new style. Sometimes, it was the Irish shanachies,[3] sometimes the French language, as he had employed it in his "Epître dédicatoire" to *The Lake*[4]:

> At this time I had been writing in different ways wondering which was better than the other. However, this epistle dedicatory was in French, and one sentence in particular pleased me, a description of the Seine and the poplars and the swallows flying low over the water. It is rather a good sentence that, though rather long. I remember I sat back and wondered to myself – "Why don't you write like that in English?" There was a good deal of use of the present participle – it doesn't do in French, though in English, and

[1] *George Moore: A Reconsideration*, Seattle (University of Washington Press) 1955, p. 27.

[2] London (Swan, Sonnenschein, Lowry) 1887, pp. 184-5, 187-8.

[3] See the opening of *Ulick and Soracha*, London (Nonesuch Press) 1926. Writers in the 1890s frequently lamented the decline of speech: Yeats evolved a philosophy of the spoken word and oral rhythms, and Moore used this.

[4] London (Heinemann) 1936. (First published in 1905; revised edn. 1921.)

99

possibly Greek, it is all right. And so it was to come about that I was to find an English style in French.[5]

Above all, it was to Wagner that he was fond of attributing his discovery of the melodic line:

> . . . It was not till I heard *Tristan* a third time that the musical pattern began to disclose itself. I went to Bayreuth again and again to hear Wagner, and to Munich to hear Wagner and Mozart, and for some years was seldom absent from the symphony concerts, where I listened with more critical ears to my old friends, Haydn, Mozart and Beethoven, thinking how a story might be woven from start to finish out of one set of ideas, each chapter rising out of the preceding chapter in suspended cadence always, never a full close.[6]

Wagner, it seems certain, gave Moore a sense of flow and implanted in him the idea of a novel approaching the condition of music; in the *Confessions* (1888) he spoke of art in terms of sequence, rhythm and harmony. Dujardin and Mallarmé[7] undoubtedly helped him to move away from Naturalism.[8] But it was chiefly to Yeats' symbolism that Moore owed his renewed search for an ideal rhythm in composition. Yeats himself was quick to point out Moore's debt:

> He did not know that style existed until he returned to

[5] Geraint Goodwin, *Conversations with George Moore*, London (Benn) 1929, p. 128.

[6] "The Nineness in the Oneness", *Century Magazine*, n.s., LXXXVII (Nov. 1919) pp. 65-6. William F. Aitken supports this claim, referring to Moore's desire for harmony of theme and smoothness of narrative, and pointing a comparison with the "Swan" motif in *Lohengrin*: see "George Moore", *Bookman*, LXXXIII, no. 498 (March, 1933), p. 488. And Harold Acton observes that the melodic line was Moore's before he consciously developed it; music was one of his closest bonds with Lady Cunard: "George Moore and the Cunard Family", *London Magazine*, vol. 5, no. 3 (March, 1958) p. 55. See also Blissett above.

[7] Mallarmé no doubt influenced his reverie: see *e.g.* Jean Noël, "George Moore et Mallarmé", *Revue de Littérature Comparée* (Jul.-Sep., 1958) p. 376; and Louis Gillet, "George Moore", *Revue des Deux Mondes*, vol. 14, 8th period (1 Apr.) 1933, p. 674.

[8] See *e.g.* John Rothenstein, *The Life and Death of Conder*, London (Dent) 1938, p. 110. Moore's whole career might be described as a movement away from realism towards reverie.

Ireland in middle life; what he learned, he learned from conversation, from acted plays, from pictures.

Collaboration with him was an unmixed misfortune for Moore, according to Yeats:

> . . . it set him upon a pursuit of style that made barren his later years.

His early years, says Yeats, gained nothing from their style; his later were written under a "misunderstanding of his powers":

> Style was his growing obsession, he would point out all the errors of some silly experiment of mine, then copy it. It was from some such experiment that he learnt those long, flaccid, structure-less sentences, "and, and and, and and" . . . Sometimes he rebelled: "Yeats, I have a deep distrust of any man who has a style," but it was generally I who tried to stop the obsession. "Moore, if you ever get a style," I would say, "it will ruin you. It is coloured glass and you need a plate-glass window." When he formed his own circle he found no escape; the difficulties of modern Irish literature . . . had been in the formation of a style. He heard these difficulties discussed . . . His nature, bitter, violent, discordant, did not fit him to write the sentences men murmur again and again for years. Charm and rhythm had been denied him. Improvement makes straight roads; he pumice-stoned every surface because will had to do the work of nature. I said once: "You work so hard that, like the Lancelot of Tennyson, you will almost see the Grail." But now, his finished work before me, I am convinced that he was denied even that "almost".[9]

Yeats, of course, was countering the charges made in *Vale*[10] that he had, in his unfortunate search for a style, ruined his later writing. Both writers thus praised each other's earlier, and criticised adversely their later work.

If Yeats was the stimulus, the actual technique of the melodic

[9] "Dramatis Personae, 1896-1902", *Autobiographies*, London (Macmillan) 1955, pp. 405-6, 437-8.
[10] See George Moore, *Vale*, London (Heinemann) 1914, pp. 165ff.

line emerged from Moore's method of dictating to his secretary draft after draft of his writing. His manner of work is worth examining in detail. He would first outline a scenario or preparatory cartoon, and divide it into chapters. Each morning he would dictate perhaps 2,000 words of "rigmarole", merely to clear his mind and get down the main ideas, so that he could see what to use and what to discard. After several more dictations, the conception of the scene, the planning of the environment, and the proportions of the chapter would begin to emerge. Only after further dictations would the words, phrases, sentence structure and imagery begin to crystallise. Often this procedure was repeated twenty times, until the final version bore no resemblance to the original skeleton. Important though dictation was, however, he insisted that it served only a preliminary function: often it was merely the incentive that enabled him to carry on. After dictation, he went over the typescript with a pen, writing and rewriting, scratching out and revising yet again. Then he would go back to his secretary and re-dictate, sometimes merely elaborating on the script but often improvising what was virtually a completely new draft. This process was repeated again and again – the description of Derby Day in *Esther Waters* was revised forty times – so that not merely the style but the structure of the story itself emerged from successive revisions. Painter friends like Ross and Blanche and scholars like Best were also called in to improve weak passages. When the proofs arrived, Moore would immediately set about revising them and, even when the book was out, he would begin altering it again for a revised edition.

This method of work was the foundation of the melodic line. Moore saw that, when one reads narrative in a book,

> one is much more acutely conscious of its transitions, interpolated retrospects, its struggling movements from one consciousness to another, than one is in listening to a story that is told orally.[11]

He realised that the English novel was too far removed from its origin in fable and

[11] Charles Morgan, "George Moore: A Centenary Appreciation", *Listener*, XLVII, no. 1200 (28 Feb. 1952) p. 351.

set himself to apply the virtues of oral narrative to the rich and complex language he had inherited from the past.[12]

"I often tell my stories far better than I write them", he told Barrett Clark.[13] He believed that a writer should never lose sight of the spoken language; otherwise he would write so pedantically that no thoughts would come. He told Eglinton at the end of his life:

No written story ever read like a spoken story, and no story ever will. Half of a spoken story is in the voice and gestures of the teller; his very presence carries the story along, and he skips over obstacles without the listener perceiving the skips. Wherefore a written story is always twice, three or four times as long as a spoken story.[14]

"As literature rises out of speech", he wrote to Nancy Cunard, "it must always retain the accent of speech; even in description of landscapes or the human mind speech should never be quite lost sight of – living speech is to literature what the wheel is to the wheelbarrow."[15] *The Lake*, with its idealisations of the rhythms of the speaking voice, bears him out. Moore's later writing is a unique blend of the spoken and the written word.

Moore was probably always inclined to reverie, a habit no doubt fostered by his solitary walks, and "imaginative reverie" seems to have its roots here. As Desmond MacCarthy says:

His genius is a genius for reverie; phase after phase in his own life or in the life of some man or woman he has known, reflection after reflection, image after image, rise, turn and evaporate like wreaths of smoke. The mood of reverie is a quiet, patient one; poignancy of emotion is foreign to it. . . . The artistic tranquillity of recollection comes easy to Mr. Moore; his difficulty has perhaps been to find sufficiently

[12] *Ibid.*

[13] Barrett Clark, *Intimate Portraits*, New York (Dramatists Play Service) 1951, p. 117.

[14] Letter to John Eglinton, 6 Jul. 1926, *Letters of George Moore*, Bournemouth (Sydenham) 1942, pp. 68-9.

[15] MS. 2648, National Library, Dublin. (Letter headed 121, Ebury Street, 8 Jan. 1926.)

strong feelings to remember. He had all his life, it seems, been more interested in examining the wrinkles in the sand left by the tide than in bathing in the sea.[16]

Moore's new style crystallised during the writing of *The Untilled Field* (1903). Then the technique of "imaginative reverie" was elaborated in *The Lake* (1905) in an attempt to solve the problem that the sole incident took place in the past. *Reminiscences of the Impressionist Painters* (1906) and *Memoirs of my Dead Life* (1906) were also retrospective. But it was in the *Hail and Farewell* autobiographical trilogy (1911-14) that Moore first worked out in detail the fictional techniques that he was to use in all his later work. He experimented with time and transitions. The opening of *Ave* is cast in the form of imaginative reverie and, throughout, the past unfolds in reverie, with meditation given the interest of narrative and imaginary incidents treated as real events. Our memories record often isolated happenings and Moore did not recreate every moment of his narrative. He adapted his material to the pattern of consciousness; he compressed, omitted and transposed. Incidents separate in time are generalised. The reader has a vivid sense of watching events as they happen, while at the same time the participant in the scene is skilfully intermingled with the later commentator. Moore broke away from the conventional techniques of autobiography. He wished to display the absurdities of the Irish Catholics, but without engaging the readers' sympathies for them by caricature. So, to justify his attacks, he indulged in self-mockery – but, of course, he selected the foibles and eccentricities he wished to mock. Another interesting feature of the structure of the trilogy is the repetition of "motifs". The journeys to Bayreuth and Ireland's sacred places

[16] *Portraits*, I, London and New York (Putnam) 1931, pp. 199-201. An interesting sidelight is thrown on this by Moore's own statement in a letter to Ross headed 121, Ebury Street, S.W., 26th June, 1913 (Margery Ross, *Robert Ross: Friend of Friends*, London [Cape] 1952, p. 243) that, if he constantly wrote plays, they would consist principally of asides and monologues:

"A man only seems natural when he is speaking aside or to himself; he seems quite mechanical when he is uttering little phrases to people standing by his elbow, as in Granville Barker's plays. Archer thinks that by suppression of asides and monologues we have advanced, but the movement is retrograde, at least it is to me."

set a pattern that was to be used in all the later books. Frequent references to Wagner's *Ring* in the first two volumes prepare us for the scene in which Moore discovers himself as Siegfried destined to restore Ireland's intellectual greatness. "Stella"[17] appears sporadically throughout the trilogy until the climax is reached. And the climax itself, the discovery of his impotence, is prepared with superb skill, merely a hint here and there throughout the trilogy until we arrive at the final revelation. All this demanded careful planning, and in the writing of *Hail and Farewell* Moore learnt a great deal about the flow of narrative.

Of the characteristics of the "melodic line", "oral narrative", and "imaginative reverie", the following are the most significant: the progressive simplification of narrative; the concern with depth rather than breadth[18]; the emphasis on unruffled narration, muted climax, suspended climax and ironic anti-climax; the anecdotes (introduced when the smoothness of the style leads to a flagging of interest) generally not so much irrelevant as tributary to the main theme[19]; the invention of ingenious episodes rather than the unravelling of complicated events; the exclusion of the author's personality, of Amico Moorini,[20] of a too personal vocabulary, and (on the whole) of humour; the lack of commitment[21]; the sacrifice, in the interests of harmony, of those stylistic contrasts, characterisation tricks, colloquialisms and individual eccentricities of character and speech which were the stock-in-trade of the Victorian novel; the smooth transitions from speech to thought, feeling, retrospect, dialogue, narrative, thought stream, action, observation, character description, and landscape –

[17] Miss Clara Christian.

[18] A river, deep and clear, was one of his favourite images.

[19] Charles Morgan (*Epitaph on George Moore*, London [Macmillan] 1935, pp. 46-7) said that anecdotes were, to Moore, windows in the corridor of narrative and exposition.

[20] Moore's name for the author of his inferior works: see *The Lake* (1921, revised edition) p. ix. The constant threat of intrusion into his mature style by Moorini, the immature young writer, was one of the most important reasons for Moore's adoption of the rule of evenness and for his lack of variation of tempo.

[21] "My work is limited to exhibition". MS 2134, National Library, Dublin (copy of letter to Edmund Gosse headed Hotel Continental, Paris, Friday 22 May 1926).

in fact, the refusal to recognise the existence of different narrative planes[22]; the languid ease of movement (sometimes degenerating into sluggishness or frozen artificiality); the shift in emphasis from realistic scene-painting to concentration on style; the avoidance of the purple patch, the passage out of key, *le mot juste* and the striking phrase; the modulated rhythms and harmony of style; the long, flowing sentences[23]; and, finally, the enormous care expended on the joining of phrase to phrase, sentence to sentence, paragraph to paragraph, and chapter to chapter, in one continuous flow. As Humbert Wolfe says:

> For him the structure of life, and therefore of art, was rhythmical. There was, he thought, an almost audible scansion in action that could and must be recaptured and recorded in the written page. The story to live must flow in and out of the rhythm of the characters. There must be no imposition of events, however picturesque, upon that inevitable flow.[24]

Thus the "melodic line", because of Moore's lack of critical terminology, is a nebulous, umbrella term, referring sometimes to narration, sometimes to stylistics. "Reverie" is equally amorphous but is used mainly to indicate the slow, meditative re-creation of past experience.

At its crudest, greater flow is merely a matter of using "and", often to excess:

> And they had gone downstairs together, and after walking about the streets in the neighbourhood of the Place de la Bourse, she proposed a cafe to him; and once out of the heat and noise of the street, some of her old liking for him had returned, though indeed she was annoyed with herself for

[22] Moore was not the first in the field here, but previous experiments had all been based on the written word.

[23] Moore read twice to Barrett Clark the MS of a much-revised preface to *In Single Strictness* (London [Heinemann] 1922). After the second reading, Clark suggested that it was too long for one sentence; to which Moore replied: "It's clear, isn't it? If a long sentence is clear it is as good as a short sentence – better. Better, I say. Without long sentences there can be no literature!" (*Intimate Portraits*, p. 75.)

[24] "Mr George Moore's Work", "The Writer", *Observer*, 22 Jan. 1933, p. 17.

having written the letter, and with him for having taken her at her word so easily.[25]

However, the device employed most frequently by Moore is the substitution, in his revised versions, of the present participle for the finite verb in an attempt to create long, flowing sentences:

> And then her thoughts passing from Harold to her mother, she remembered the pain that his mother's failings used to cause Harold during the last years of her life; for there was no denying that her mother often drank more wine than was good for her, and when that happened her tongue was unrestrained – she talked with her butler during dinner about the cedars of Lebanon; and though Harold admired his mother's contributions to the *Saturday Review*, he could not bring himself to accept them as sufficient atonement for her social transgressions.[26]

Comparison of the following passages from the 1905 and 1921 editions of *The Lake* reveals how the jerky style of the original is transformed by a characteristic addition of "and", "but", "for" and the present participle:

> . . . for a while. But he had never been out of sight of this lake except the years he had spent in Maynooth. When he left Maynooth he had pleaded that he might be sent to live among the mountains by Kilronan Abbey at the north end of the lake . . . when Father Conway died he had been moved round to the western shore. Every day in his life he walked by the lake; there was nowhere else to walk. . . .

> . . . for a while, and he had only been out of sight of this lake in the years he spent in Maynooth. On leaving he had pleaded that he might be sent to live among the mountains by Kilronan Abbey, at the north end of the lake, but when Father Conway died he was moved round to the western

[25] "Henrietta Marr", *Celibate Lives*, Ebury Edition, London (Heinemann) 1937, pp. 144-5. This book, whose final revision was published in 1927, was a revised version of *In Single Strictness*, which was in turn a completely rewritten version of *Celibates*, London (Scott) 1895.

[26] *Op. cit.*, pp. 101-2.

shore; and every day since he walked by the lake, for there
was nowhere else to walk. . . .[27]

In this way, short sentences are constantly combined into longer
ones:

Mildred looked at the cold face, so claylike, and trembled.
The horror of the situation crept over her; she had no
strength to go, and listened meekly to Ellen.

Etta looked at the cold face, so clay-like, and the horror of
the situation creeping over her, she lost strength to go, and
listened meekly to Ellen.[28]

Sometimes sentences are even distorted to produce greater flow:

Of landing places there seemed to be no sign.

. . . into which it was nearly time they should jump.

Out of whose toothless gums. . . .[29]

Whereas vocabulary is sometimes simplified in the revised
versions – as in *The Brook Kerith* – construction is often complicated to obtain long, periodic sentences. And as with the sentence,
so with the paragraph: the first seven paragraphs of chapter one
of the 1916 edition of *The Brook Kerith* are reduced to one in the
1927 edition, the eighteen in this chapter to four, the twenty-eight
in the second chapter to six, and the fifteen in the fourth chapter
to three.

Equally important in Moore's later writing is the device of
repetition to cement together narrative, speech, and description.
With great skill the prose of the following passage is bound
together by the changes rung on the words "Long Hand the
Guff", "jailer", "demon", "damned soul", "hell", "stream",
"ruined castle", "key", "punishment", and "burning":

She was giving him the usual religious instruction, hell, of
course, figuring largely in it, and he had asked her if being
burnt for ever hurt as much as being burnt for a short time.

[27] *The Lake*, London (Heinemann) 1905, pp. 6-7; revised edition 1921, p. 5.
[28] "Mildred Lawson", *Celibates*, p. 145; "Henrietta Marr", *Celibate Lives*,
p. 127.   [29] "Hugh Monfert", *In Single Strictness*, pp. 116, 117.

He knew nothing about burning at the time and his mother had laughed; and encouraged by her laughter he said: Is there no other punishment but burning in hell? Oh yes, she had answered, and told him a little story – that one of the punishments of hell was the hopelessness of ever getting out of hell, and so that this torment of hope might be stimulated, the damned were allowed to try to get out of hell, to steal the keys. He had asked his mother where the keys were, and she told him of a ruined castle some miles from the main road, reached by a narrow lane, and that it was in this castle that the jailer of the damned dwelt. There was a little stream across the road over which the jailer was not allowed to pass, and the damned soul knew that if he could hit off the time when the jailer was having his dinner, he could take the keys from the rail on which they hung. The soul crawled along the little walls so that none should see him; once he had crossed the bridge he was in the power of the demon that lived in the ruined tower, and when he got under the walls of the castle his plan was to cry out: Long Hand the Guff, are you there? If he cried three times he might be sure that Long Hand the Guff was away upon some other business. But Long Hand the Guff kept a good watch and before the soul had cried out for the third time: Long Hand the Guff, are you there? the demon was out of the ruined castle, and the soul fled, knowing that if he could only reach the stream he would be safe. But every moment Long Hand the Guff would gain upon him, till at last he would feel the great arm stretching out to seize him, and just as he put his foot into the water the hand would clasp about his neck and drag him back. None had ever escaped Long Hand the Guff. If he had asked his mother what punishment Long Hand the Guff put the soul to in the ruined castle he could not remember, but the flight of the soul from the ruined castle to the brook and the coming stench of the demon upon the unfortunate soul had sunk into his mind.[30]

The "dream" passage in this short story is characteristic in its repetition of Moore's favourite imagery:

[30] *Op. cit.*, pp. 138-9.

Those dawn dreams shake one's nerves, said Hugh; and strange to say I, who rarely dream, dreamed last night. We were very tired and for a long time we must have lain dozing; dreams, it is said, come just before waking. I wish I could remember my dream – something about a hermitage; for me it was one, though it was filled with eighteenth century furniture. You were dreaming of Wotton Hall, said Percy.[31]

Repetition of a word, phrase or material object to obtain cohesion is employed frequently in the 1921 *Lake*. There is an excellent illustration of this in the repetition of "river", "traditions and symbols", "belief", and "merit" in the description of the scholar Poole:

> ... Mr. Walter Poole's conversation was usually gentle, like a quiet river, and very often, like a quiet river, it rushed rapidly when Mr. Walter Poole became interested in his subject. "How very superior all this is," the priest said. "The river of thought in him," the interviewer continued, "is deep or shallow, according to the need of the moment. If, for instance, Mr. Walter Poole is asked if he be altogether sure that it is wise to disturb people in the belief in the traditions and symbols that have held sway for centuries, he will answer quickly that if truth lies behind the symbols and traditions, it will be in the interest of the symbols and traditions to inquire out the truth, for blind belief – in other words, faith – is hardly a merit, or if it be a merit it is a merit that cannot be denied to the savages who adore idols."[32]

Moore, in his revisions of his novels, took pains to introduce this device, as we may see from a comparison of the 1905 and 1921 versions of *The Lake*:

> 1905: But what had he done in spite of Father Peter's warning ...
> 1921: ... but unable to resist that beguiling tongue, for Mrs. O'Hara had a beguiling tongue.

> 1905: He gashed his chin, however, for he could not keep his attention fixed on his work.

31 *Op. cit.*, p. 100.
32 *The Lake* (1921) pp. 97-8.

1921: . . . gashing his chin, however, for he could not keep
his attention fixed on his chin.[33]

Such repetition of a material object to keep it in our minds is
particularly frequent in his later work:

> . . . thinking of her bathroom and the comfort of it, remem-
> bering that in the hotel in the Quartier Latin there was no
> bathroom, and that she and Cissie and Elsie had had to go to
> some public baths, a thing that she disliked to do. Bathing,
> she had said, where all the bodies in the town have been . . .
> Etta turned over and over, thinking how pleasant it was to
> go straight from one's bedroom to one's bath; and returning
> from her bath in a white wrapper. . . .[34]

Repetition of proper names is employed in the same manner –
Gerard de Rousillon and the Emperor in "Hugh Monfert,[35]"
O'Grady in The Lake,[36] L'Homme Masqué in the following passage
from "Henrietta Marr":

> And then it began to be noticed, Davau said, that I dis-
> appeared from the auditorium when "L'Homme Masqué"
> was in the arena, and to show that I was not "L'Homme
> Masqué" I took a seat in full view of the public; and on that
> very night it so happened that "L'Homme Masqué" only
> just escaped defeat. The man who was nearly overthrown was
> your cousin, Etta interjected. You were "L'Homme
> Masqué" in turns.[37]

Over-used, this is a wearisome trick, and it is interesting that
what later became a deliberately introduced stylistic device began
as a looseness in construction – compare the following passages
from the 1905 and 1921 editions of The Lake:

> . . . perched on an alder bush; the bush was the only one
> amid a bed of flags and rushes.

> . . . perched on a bush, the only one among a bed of flags and
> rushes; "an alder bush," he said.[38]

---

[33] Op. cit., p. 33 (1905); p. 23 (1921); p. 47 (1905); pp. 32-3 (1921).
[34] "Henrietta Marr", p. 104.   [35] "Hugh Monfert", p. 158.
[36] The Lake (1921), p. 78.   [37] "Henrietta Marr", p. 131.
[38] The Lake, p. 9 (1905); p. 7 (1921).

The hunt metaphor in *The Lake* throws further light on Moore's methods:

> 1905 : And to live on, never seeing her or ever hearing from her seemed to him the most unbearable lot that could have fallen to his share. The hunt was over, and the spoil lay hearing with dying ears the horns calling to each other in the echoing distances.

> 1921 : The grave is dreamless! But there might be a long time before he reached it, living for years without seeing or even hearing from her, for she would weary of writing to him. He began to dream of a hunt, the quarry hearing with dying ears the horns calling to each other in the distance . . .[39]

In the later version, the personalisation of the hunt, the introduction of dreams, the repetition of "dream" and "hearing" and the effective use of assonance ("dre*a*mless", "re*a*ched", "ye*a*rs", "s*ee*ing", "he*a*ring", "we*a*ry", "dream", "e*a*rs", "e*a*ch") create a fine passage of tightly-knit prose.

Another of Moore's devices for binding together the narrative more closely and achieving an unbroken story-line is the introduction of a fresh thought into the last part of a sentence:

> Her forgiveness had brought real relief; but Miss Glynn said in her letter that she was alone in Berkshire, Mr. Poole having gone to London to seek information regarding the altars of the early Israelites.[40]

> But there, she had neither his skill nor his strength, not even strength to pull on her stockings, only just enough to pull them off and roll herself into bed again and rest, which she did, lying between sleeping and waking till the maid knocked at her door and handed her a letter from Elsie.

> And the three marched across the grass plot, their arms about each other's waists, and whilst questioning Etta about herself and telling her about themselves, they frequently looked where their lovers sat smoking, Etta's attention drawn to a

---

[39] *Op. cit.*, pp. 234-5 (1905); p. 135 (1921).
[40] *Op. cit.*, p. 81 (1921).

girl who hung over Morton, desirous that he should listen
only to her.[41]

Then there is the abrupt ending of a cadence on an open
monosyllable:

> Oliver was in command of the raiders, and at first he seems
> to have been successful; he pillaged and burnt every town,
> gathering a large booty wherever he went, till a great host of
> Saracens surrounded his army; but Roland and the Crusaders
> came to his rescue, despite their belief that they would never
> see the light of another day.[42]

But "flow" is not merely a matter of stylistics, and the "melodic
line" introduces major changes in narrative technique. One of
the most significant narrative devices used by Moore is the muting
of a climax, the deliberate, sometimes ironic anticlimax. A good
illustration of this occurs in the 1921 *Lake* where there has been
a long build-up to the introduction of Nora into the conversation
between O'Grady and Gogarty; at the moment when we expect
the culmination, Moore plays down the introduction of the vital
factor. O'Grady's departure is another effective suspended
cadence: it is not stated directly – merely, "till the car came round
to take Father O'Grady away",[43] followed immediately by
Gogarty's meditations. In "Hugh Monfert", the wedding of Hugh
and Beatrice is dismissed in a phrase, the muted climax underlining
the central theme of the novel: it is the Hugh-Percy, not the
Hugh-Beatrice relationship with which we are concerned.

Even more significant is Moore's management of transitions.
Changes of plane from narrative to thought and on to speech and
reminiscence are smooth and unbroken:

> He had always looked upon his mother as the most unselfish
> of women, and to find her one of the most selfish frightened
> him; and his thoughts passing on he was drawn to seek
> excuses for her willingness to sacrifice his happiness. She is
> some years over fifty, and if she is to enjoy her grandchildren
> no time must be lost; that is her point of view, and she is so

---

[41] "Henrietta Marr", pp. 133-4, 136.
[42] "Hugh Monfert", p. 130.
[43] *The Lake* (1921) p. 94.

absorbed in her dream of grandchildren that she forgets me.
He laughed aloud and repeated her words: You are the last.
Her passion for grandchildren could be nothing else than it
is, he added, for she married that the family might linger on
for another couple of hundred years, having no thought for
the fact that everything ends sooner or later, even the
glorious name of Montferrat. And his thoughts deviating a
little, he remembered her father, Joe Huxtable . . .[44]

The delight in long, weaving sentences, the subtle changes of
plane from narrative to dialogue and thought-stream to retrospect, and the smooth changes of speaker, are seen perhaps at their
best in this story:

But Hugh could not be shaken out of his lethargy, coma,
stupor, whatever it was; he lay back inert and all Percy could
get out of him was: I can't go over that story today, half of
it is forgotten, Percy; my brain will not work. Whereupon
Percy watched Hugh's great broad face, his long, loose
mouth and his vague, shifting eyes, saying: I shall get
nothing out of him today. It is strange, he added, to lie
without seeing or hearing, and yet awake.

Percy's restless mind, plain upon his thin, pale face, was
able to penetrate Hugh's almost animal indolence, now and
again stirred by remembrance of Stanislaus College; the
great, red-brick tower in which a bell tolled, bringing them
to lessons and to play, the long narrow passage down which
he was sent to the prefect's room to be flogged . . .[45]

Morning passes into luncheon without apparent break, and
speeches merge into one another. Changes of plane and person
are skilfully introduced, and transitions are smooth, even where
there is a paragraph division:

But do you think, Beatrice asked, that Percy is at present old
enough – Has enough command of his talent? Hugh interjected. Indeed I do.

And the girl sat listening, her long thin hand (so like
Percy's, Hugh thought) laid upon the open book, her eyes
awake like Percy's when a thought flashed into her mind.

[44] "Hugh Monfert", p. 48.   [45] Op. cit., p. 137.

Her thoughts do not move so quickly as his, he said to himself, but they move; and he continued to praise the drawings that Percy had made, taking note of the intellectual stir upon her face, a flushed face, shadowed with bright brown hair. A prettier face than Percy's, not so thin, but of the same cast of countenance, he thought during a pause that had fallen upon them. You have seen him draw then? Beatrice asked.[46]

The revised *Lake*, too, excels here. The following passage contains an excellent transition from speech to narrative, narrative to reverie and reverie to the magazine article projected through Gogarty's consciousness:

"I suppose it isn't fair", the priest said, "to judge a man through his interviewer; but if this interviewer doesn't misrepresent Mr. Walter Poole, Mr. Walter Poole is what is commonly known as a very superior person. He would appear from this paper," the priest said, "to be a man between thirty and forty, not many years older than myself." The priest's thoughts floated away back into the past, and, returning suddenly with a little start to the present, he continued reading the interview, learning from it that Mr. Walter Poole's conversation was usually gentle . . .[47]

Transitions between letter and narrative are also subtle and varied in this edition. And in all the later works nature description is threaded in skilfully with thought and dialogue. The Welsh landscape in "Hugh Monfert" permeates the boys' experiences, and the beautiful view seen by Monfert and Dr Knight in the evening at Wotton Hall is woven in with Hugh's state of mind. Transitions between chapters are also smooth in Moore's later writing: a comparison of "Mildred Lawson" and "Henrietta Marr" chapter endings proves particularly illuminating.

Moore was proud of his ability to write exposition and some of his later works are superb. "Hugh Monfert", for example, begins with a tightly-knit first chapter largely in the form of reminiscence while Hugh is shaving. We learn of Knight's coming down to mediate between Hugh and his mother concerning an heir. Contemplation of the motives for his mother's willingness to

sacrifice his happiness leads naturally on to details of her background – in particular, her father, Joe Huxtable (a rich peasant
who married her to the aristocratic Monfert), Hugh's childhood,
her husband, her redemption of the estate from debt and the
financial reasons for his not going to Oxford. All this might now
be wasted, and so we return to Knight as the mediator. The
compression, economy and unity here are remarkable, with
smooth transitions from present to past, action to reminiscence:
"and once more forgetful of his shaving . . ."; ". . . and his
thoughts passing on . . ."; ". . . and his thoughts deviating a
little, he remembered . . ."; ". . . and he began to consider . . .";
". . . and he continued in his thought . . ."; ". . . and to atone for
the thought that had come into his mind unasked, he dwelt
on . . ."; ". . . and he remembered . . ."; ". . . and the image of
himself and his mother . . . rose up in his thoughts clear and
distinct. He could still hear her voice if he listened for it . . .";
". . . and he stood, razor in hand, appalled by the calamity";
". . . and he thought of . . ."; ". . . All I ask (and again he began
to shave himself) . . ."; ". . . A sudden sense of the humour of this
quarrel obliged him to stop shaving, and whilst thinking . . . he
recalled . . ."; ". . . and he stood thinking . . ."; ". . . stopping on
the staircase . . ." and so on.[48] Moore does not continue too long
with the facts; the story of Joe Huxtable is broken soon with,
"Such thoughts as these must have come to his grandfather . . ."
Questions, too, help to maintain the illusion: "Was it the desire
to raise herself socially? It may have been that . . ."[49] The whole
is an excellent illustration of the melodic line.

Another means of improving narrative flow is the introduction
of phrases to render speech and thought through the consciousness of the characters. It is interesting to note how this device,
coupled with a tightening of the structure, omission of the
repetitive "vaguely", and the substitution of a present participle
for a finite verb, increases the continuity of the following passage
from *The Lake*:

> 1905: The earth and sky were enfolding in one tender
>   harmony of rose and blue, the blue shading down to
>   gray, and the lake floated amid vague shores, vaguely

[48] "Hugh Monfert", pp. 47-53.   [49] *Op. cit.*, p. 49.

as a dream floats through sleep. The swallows were flying high, quivering overhead in the blue air. There was a sense of security and persuasion and loveliness in the evening.

1921: And he watched the earth and sky enfolded in one tender harmony of rose and blue – blue fading to grey, and the lake afloat amid vague shores, receding like a dream through sleep.[50]

There are in *The Lake* many such beautiful passages of "thought blended with sense; and sense sunken in thought".[51] The "fountain speech" in particular is a superb illustration of how Moore bound together narrative, reflexion and speech, projecting the whole through Gogarty's consciousness:

His thoughts melted into nothingness, and when he awoke from his reverie he was thinking that Norah Glynn had come into his life like a fountain, shedding living water upon it, awakening it. And taking pleasure in the simile, he said, "A fountain better than anything else expresses this natural woman," controlled, no doubt, by a law, but one hidden from him. "A fountain springs out of earth into air; it sings a tune that cannot be caught and written down in notes; the rising and falling water is full of iridescent colour, and to the wilting roses the fountain must seem not a natural thing, but a spirit, and I, too, think of her as a spirit." And his thoughts falling away again he became vaguely but intensely conscious of all the beauty and grace and the enchantment of the senses that appeared to him in the name of Nora Glynn.[52]

One final aspect of the melodic line must be mentioned: Moore's later narrative device of enriching the story with "myths". This is well illustrated by "Hugh Monfert", where there are, in addition to slighter references, four main ones: the stories of Ferabras, Long Hand the Guff, Gerard de Rousillon, and

[50] *The Lake* (1905), p. 268; (1921), pp. 156-7. See also (1905), pp. 271-2; (1921), pp. 158-9.

[51] John Freeman, *A Portrait of George Moore in a Study of his Work*, London (Laurie) 1922, p. 169.

[52] *The Lake* (1921) pp. 151-2.

Floripar and Guy of Burgundy.[53] These myths are told with great zest, are skilfully woven into the narrative and are made relevant by the "monolithic" style, the manner of their introduction and their relation to the central character: Ferabras deals with belief in miracles, Long Hand the Guff with the stultifying effects of Catholicism, Gerard de Rousillon with physical and spiritual love, and Floripar with love and purity. In this way they are made acceptable to the reader.

Moore's "melodic line" narration is to be seen perhaps at its best in a short story, "Priscilla and Emily Lofft",[54] first published in book form in *In Single Strictness* and later in *Celibate Lives*. In the Advertisement to *Celibate Lives*,[55] Moore wrote that "Priscilla and Emily Lofft" was a story of "two sisters – spinsters, one because of her devotion to her sister, the other from lack of sex impulse – and the characteristics of the two sisters are enshrined in a pathetic little story". The sisters, leading sheltered lives, living together and reading the same books, have their first and only misunderstanding when, by accident, a copy of *Emma Bovary* falls into the hands of one of them, revealing to her something of the life she has missed, and only after her death is her secret discovered by her sister.

The keynote is a gentle, Turgenev-like pathos, well suited to the tranquil melancholy of faded lives. The blackbird immediately sets the tone, and Moore's characteristic style is seen to perfection in the long first sentence:

> A blackbird whistled in the garden when Emily flung the drawing-room door open and gazed into the emptiness of the old faded room, her eyes falling straightway upon a portrait painted in clear tones of two children sitting on a green bank overshadowed by trees, turning the leaves of a picture book, twins, seemingly, so like were they one to the other,

[53] The habit of inserting stories from literature into his work is present in Moore from his very first novel, *A Modern Lover* (1883). No doubt this tendency is linked up with the often naive enthusiasm with which Moore rushed to tell everyone of each new discovery he made. Wilde mocked him for carrying on his education in public.

[54] This was a revised version of "Emma Bovary", which appeared in *Lippincott's Monthly Magazine*, vol. 69 (May 1902), pp. 589-95.

[55] See Barrett Clark, p. 116.

light-hearted girls, with brown ringlets showering about their faces.[56]

The drawing-room to which Emily returns after her sister's funeral brings memories flooding back into her mind, and her aunts are skilfully introduced by means of their paintings on the walls. Memory, thought and speech are woven together:

> . . . had she lived another two months, all would have been changed; and Emily asked herself if it would be harder for her to live in a new house, a house repapered, repainted, and refurnished, a house that would bear no memory of Priscilla, or to live in this old house in which her sister's presence lingered like a ghost. Every piece of furniture, every picture, reminded her of something she had said to Priscilla or Priscilla had said to her. If that bird would only cease, she muttered, and fell to thinking that she had hated to hear him sing on the day that Priscilla died.[57]

A blackbird had sung on the day they came to Dublin as children, and the bird provides a good transition to the story of their early life, their arrival as orphans in Dublin when they were ten years old. There follows a description and history of the garden, in which they are finally allowed to play. Emily returns to her present grief, and then the blackbird whistling outside reminds her of her schooldays, and the Reverend Mother's remark about the difference in ability between her and her sister. Their likeness is dwelt on and this leads smoothly to the memory of their being dressed similarly, when older, by Mrs Symond, which in turn opens the way naturally to the relation of Emily's spinsterhood, the breaking off of her engagement with James Mease as he would not allow Priscilla to live with them, and the cause of Priscilla's death – because of the scandal they had to go to the country, where Priscilla caught a cold. A new thought now enters Emily's mind: perhaps Priscilla wishes her to stay in Dublin to remember her. Consideration of her reason for remaining introduces another excellent transition:

> Lonely evenings, she said, the words provoked by the sight of the books in the bookcase . . .[58]

---

[56] *Celibate Lives*, p. 26.   [57] *Op. cit.*, p. 27.   [58] *Op. cit.*, p. 33.

and so their reading is brought in. The books they have read together remind her of the death, the doctor, his recommending the south again, and the details of Priscilla's illness. She remembers having met a friend coming from the house and, on being told that Priscilla was ill, she decided to get a doctor, but the next day Priscilla was dead, and Emily tries to forget her struggle for breath. Then she recalls that Priscilla died striving for speech: pencil and paper were brought, but she failed to write, and Emily wonders about the secret, for they had never hidden anything from each other.

> What could it be? They had never been separated; only at Aix had they ever occupied different rooms. And her thoughts passing out of Dublin . . .[59]

– so we learn of the stay in France, the separate bedrooms, Priscilla's preference for this state of affairs, her hiding some object beneath her pillow, and Emily's present deduction that this, their sole misunderstanding, must be connected with the mystery. Narrative and dialogue are skilfully mingled:

> . . . the proprietress warned them that they would find it very hard to get a double-bedded room in any of the hotels. It being the height of the season, she said, you may not be able to get a room at all. And have to sleep in the streets, Emily whispered to Priscilla, forgetful that the proprietress spoke English. The nights are very cold, the proprietress answered, and the thought of the danger that a cold night might be to Priscilla compelled her to accept the two rooms . . .[60]

The scribbled words "in the garden" are now cleverly introduced. Because she may never find a solution, Emily wonders whether she will ever be less unhappy than she is now, and this leads naturally on to her friends' consolations, the story of her life since Priscilla's death, the gradual spiritualising of her grief and Priscilla's presence in the room or emergence from the potting shed. Sometimes, it seems that she is asking for Emily's help, and it is Emily's powerlessness that keeps her in Dublin, because she feels that a secret will be revealed to her. Years pass until one day a shower drives Emily to the potting shed and she finds

[59] *Op. cit.*, p. 35.   [60] *Ibid.*

the novel and the dictionary, realising that she has discovered the secret. Details of the story are told naturally, and a former conversation is skilfully woven in. Finally, Emily's piecing together of Priscilla's motives for reading the book and for her subsequent secrecy is masterly: she knew no man who could have given it her – so Priscilla must have found it – in her bedroom at Aix – a previous occupant must have left it – but the housemaids would see it – so it must have fallen behind a chest of drawers – but why did Priscilla bring it to England? – because she could not give it to the proprietress or leave it behind without tarnishing her reputation, and there were no fires to burn it – she was too ashamed to confess to Emily that she had read it, and therefore had to carry it to England – so Priscilla's spirit had kept Emily there to burn the book. The book is sacrificially burnt, Emily is freed, and she goes to bed as the blackbird whistles in the dusk.

The economy here is remarkable: every detail counts. Told largely in retrospect, "Priscilla and Emily Lofft" skilfully mingles action with speech, narrating the story through Emily's consciousness and thus ensuring a tight unity and coherence. Its greatest merit is the beautiful, slow unfolding of the story by means of subtle transitions from one narrative plane to another, from past to present and back again to past. It is a superb example of Moore's later story-telling.

The "melodic line" took shape in *The Untilled Field* (1903) and *The Lake* (1905), was refined in *Hail and Farewell* (1911-14), and blossomed in *The Brook Kerith* (1916), *Héloïse and Abélard* (1921), the revised *Lake* (1921) and *In Single Strictness* (1922). In works such as these Moore achieves a narrative mode unique in prose fiction.

Bonamy Dobrée

GEORGE MOORE'S FINAL WORKS

In the conversation with Whittaker[1] that prefaces his *Daphnis and Chloë* of 1924, George Moore says: "I am not without subjects; my head is full of subjects for books; but I cannot bring myself to write one of them." His friend suggests that he should try translation, as a result of which advice Moore tackled Longus, having already – to judge from the talk – plunged deeply into scholarly research as to the manuscripts.

But before retreating into translation he had had an intermediate phase, in which, not inventing, ordering, writing as he had done in his earlier books such as *Esther Waters*, he had taken classic subjects, treating them in so wide a manner that his books have been referred to as Epics. Yet this seems hardly an appropriate name for them, apart from their not being in verse – though they are "poetic" enough – since Moore was not so much interested in the deeds of his main figures, or their effect on the world around them, as in their thoughts and the philosophic ideas current in their day. He put considerable research into this also, and his conversation with Whittaker opens with him saying: "Whilst I wrote *The Brook Kerith*, we talked of the Gospels and the Epistles, of Josephus, Philo-Judæus, and Apollonius of Tyana; and when I was writing *Héloïse and Abélard* we talked of Duns Scotus Erigena of the ninth century, of the Realists and Nominalists of the twelfth. We have talked so much philosophy and Greek literature . . ." to a degree that in a sense the narrative thread of the novels fades in importance before the discussion of ideas.

[1] T. W. Whittaker, a well-known writer on neo-platonism, and Director of the Rationalist Press Association, to whom Moore used to submit his scripts.

This is not to say that the people do not matter; they do, fundamentally, though not so much from their acts as from the emotion-thoughts that direct these acts. Thus these novels consist largely of discussion about, say, imagination and reality, Realism and Nominalism, indeed a number of the conflicting notions that in various forms, under various names, run perpetually through the minds of human beings. Moore does this in a very individual way, showing a host of differing people in stories so complex that "thou must read from the beginning and not skip, else thou'll miss the chief beauty, the unfolding of the story, clouds arising out of clouds and melting into clouds", as Héloïse tells her uncle Fulbert about reading Virgil. And as you read these later works you are enthralled by "the beautiful voice that [brings] out sentence after sentence, like silk from a spool", – as the speech of Mathias is described in *The Brook Kerith*. It is this language, seeming to unwind itself phrase after sustained phrase, rather than "thou" and "hath", that gives these final works their distance in time, their remoteness from present-day reality, as the dates of the stories demand. It is suitable for the mundane or matter-of-fact, the splendid description, or the philosophic aphorism; and, moreover, binds together the complex story, or, rather, stories – "clouds arising out of clouds".

The Brook Kerith (1916) is essentially a religious book, centrally an unorthodox life of Christ. It opens with a charmingly sympathetic account of the boyhood of Joseph of Arimathea, in many ways the ordinary happy youngling, who enjoys watching sheep, bird-nesting, and egg-collecting, and is seduced from his lessons by meeting on the way to his teacher wandering groups of cock-fighters or strolling players. But when he was very young his grandmother had told him the story of Samuel and Saul; and that night he dreamt that Samuel appeared to him. When he tells this to his father Dan, a rich salted-fish merchant of Magdala in Galilee, and learns that Samuel is supposed to be their ancestor, he goes into more detail, saying that he had seen the face as one "that a spirit might wear, for it was not made up of flesh but of some glowing matter or stuff, such as glow-worms are made of. . ." From that time he had a burning desire for knowledge, of the Hebrew his forefathers spoke and in which the Scriptures were written, and soon for Greek, that he might know what the

Greeks thought. After some unsatisfactory teachers he comes
under the tutelage of Azariah, a man of wide general learning.

We soon get a taste of the qualities that run through these
books, of the philosophic element, as, when Azariah is taking
Joseph to Arimathea to try to find the place where Samuel met
Saul, the pupil is told: "It is hard to do good without doing
wrong to another", or of the descriptive passages, very short here,
when, for instance they approach the place:

> The town was an enchantment in the still limpid morning,
> but when they rose to their feet their eyes fell on a greater
> enchantment – the hills clothed in moving light and shade
> so beautiful that the appeal to come away to the woods and
> fields continued in their hearts after they had lowered their
> eyes and would not be denied, though they prayed for
> strength to hold by their original project . . .[2]

namely, to study and ponder over the story of David and Goliath.

Azariah becomes a kind of god-father to the boy, arousing the
father's jealousy, Dan being delighted when Joseph tires of his
teacher, and plunges into the business of salt-fish trading, gets
to know the fishermen, has ideas for expanding the trade, and
shows himself to be a good administrator. The direction of the
story appears when Joseph takes his father's place in making the
Passover visit to Jerusalem. He goes there as a good Pharisee, but
finds that the Pharisees are too much given to strict observance of
the Law, and is disgusted with the scepticism of the Sadducees
and their sacrifice of animals. Then he hears of the Essenes, who
deemed "the shedding of blood a crime. A still more fundamental
tenet of this sect was its denial of private property: all they had
belonged to one brother as much as to another", and they dis-
dained marriage: a "cheerful exclusion of all pleasure from life
seemed to Joseph wonderful, an exaltation of the spirit that he
had not hitherto believed man to be capable of". So he makes his
way to the cenoby near Jericho, where first he is plunged into
philosophic discourse with Mathias, who had spent many years in
Alexandria and become an enthusiastic follower of Heraclitus.
But the important point of a picturesquely detailed narrative is
Joseph's meeting with an Essene shepherd, Jesus, who had been

[2] *The Brook Kerith*, London (Heinemann) 1927 (final version), p. 20.

baptised by John, and his being struck by "the fine brow curving upwards – a noble arch he said to himself – eyes mysterious as stars, and a certain underlying sadness in the voice, oftentimes soft and low but with a cry in it occasionally".

But he loses sight of Jesus; hears he has gone to Egypt and, undergoing periods of deep depression, seeks him there, spending two years away from home, to his father's distress. When he does go home he finds there Jesus, who had gone back to Galilee, the country of his origin, who tells him: "A man travels the world over in search of what he needs and returns home to find it." Jesus has formed a little group consisting of Dan's fishermen, the simple-minded Simon Peter, James, and John, and others, such as Matthew. Can Joseph as the son of a rich man join them? There is great discussion about this; and another point that makes his reception among them dubious is that he is a philosopher, and Jesus told him "that philosophies change in different men, but the love of God is the same in all men". But what finally prevents Joseph from becoming one of the apostles is that he deserts them to tend his father who is dangerously ill. While watching over Dan he ruminates at great length, among other things remembering the Greek philosopher who said: "Reality is but an eternal shaping and reshaping of things", and that "all men bring a different sensitiveness into the world, knowledge is a word without meaning, for there can be no knowledge".

His father recovers, and he meets Jesus again, now faced with the prospect of his ordeal in Jerusalem. He finds him

> very different from the severe young man he had seen in the monastery. He had grown older, more careworn, but the first Jesus still lingered in the second, whereas the Jesus he was looking at now was a new Jesus, one whom he had never seen before; the cheeks had fallen in and the eyes that he remembered, soft and luminous, were now concentrated; a sort of malignant hate glowered in them: he seemed to hate all he looked upon; and his features seemed to have been enlarged, the nose and chin were more prominent, and the body was shrunken.[3]

Jesus upbraids him violently, "telling him that there was no place

Op. cit., p. 182.

among his followers for those who could not free themselves from such ghosts as father, mother and children and wife".

Nevertheless he goes to Jerusalem when Jesus does, and after the crucifixion, Joseph, on good terms with Pilate, asks permission to take the corpse of Jesus, who has been reported dead after very few hours, and gets to Golgotha in time to bribe the Roman soldier not to pierce the side: "Do not insult the dead", he says. He has the body taken to his own tomb, and places it there without rolling the stone to close it. When he goes back to do so he finds that Jesus is alive, carries him to his home, and, after concealing him for some days, takes him down to the Essenes. It is in the Essene cenoby that Moore develops his idea of one-ness with God.

So much for the main outlines of the story. What gives the book its enthralling quality is the way it is told, giving us the pondered thoughts of the people, and the physical setting as it affects the characters. It is as though Moore wanted us to sense the whole man at any given instant, not the thought alone but the feelings, too – the ideas, the hopes, the regrets, the immediate apprehension. A quotation may illustrate this, a long one, since quotations from this work tend to be long, for one hesitates to break the silk as it unwinds from the spool.

One evening, while looking after Dan, Joseph goes out for a little and sees the stars:

> Behind the stars that twinkled were stars that blazed; behind the stars that blazed were smaller stars, and behind them a sort of luminous dust. All this immensity is God's dwelling-place, he said. The stars are God's eyes; we live under his eyes and he has given us a beautiful garden to live in. Are we worthy of it? he asked; and Jew though he was he forgot God for a moment, in the sweetness of the breathing of earth, for there is no more lovely plain in the spring of the year than the Plain of Gennesaret.
>
> Every breath of air brought a new and exquisite scent to him, and through the myrtle bushes he could hear the streams singing their way down to the lake; and when he came to the lake's edge he heard the warble that came into his ear when he was a little child, which it retained always. He heard it in

Egypt, under the Pyramids, and the cataracts of the Nile were not able to silence it in his ears. But suddenly from among the myrtle bushes a song arose. It began with a little phrase of three notes, which the bird repeated, as if to impress the listener and prepare him for the runs and trills and joyous little cadenzas that were to follow. A sudden shower of jewels it seemed like, and when the last drops had fallen the bird began another song, a continuation of the first, but more voluptuous and intense; and then, as if he felt that he had set the theme sufficiently, he started away into new trills and shakes and runs, piling cadenza upon cadenza till the theme seemed lost, but the bird held it in memory while all its musical extravagances were flowing, and when the inevitable moment came he repeated the first three notes. Again Joseph heard the warbling water, and it seemed to him that he could hear the stars throbbing. It was one of those moments when the soul of man seems to break, to yearn for that original unity out of which some sad fate has cast it – a moment when the world seems to be one thing and not several things: the stars and the stream, the odours afloat upon the stream, the bird's song and the words of Jesus: Whoever admires the stars and flowers finds God in his heart, seemed to become all blended into one extraordinary harmony; and unable to resist the emotion of the moment any longer, Joseph threw himself upon the ground and prayed that the moment he was living in might not be taken from him, but that it might endure for ever. But while he prayed the moment was passing, and becoming suddenly aware that it had gone, he rose from his knees and returned home mentally weary and sad at heart; but sitting on his bedside the remembrance that he was to meet Jesus in the morning at Capernaum called up the ghost of a departed ecstasy, and his head drowsing upon his pillow he fell asleep, hushed by remembrances.[4]

The theme of the last third of *The Brook Kerith* is the finding of God, or of the idea of God as pursued by Jesus, so passionately that it is as though Moore himself were impelled to this quest.

[4] *Op. cit.*, pp. 123-4.

We are again transported to a cenoby of the Essenes; for now there are two, one accepting marriage because only so can the number of Essenes be maintained. But the attempt at joyless breeding failed, as might be imagined, and no children are born. "Our dream", one of them confesses, "was to perpetuate holiness in this world, and our dream abides, for man is a reality only in his dreams; his acts are but a grotesque of this dream." The others reject marriage, since "woman represents the five senses: pleasure of the eyes, of the ears, of the mouth, of the fingertips, of the nostrils", and, moreover, "sexual pleasure leads to the pleasure of wine and food". They have removed themselves to a cave-like dwelling on a rocky ledge near the Brook Kerith. When Jesus gets to this latter cenoby, he finds that an old shepherd there is getting beyond the work, and he offers to take it on, to the delight of the Essenes. So he resumes an old duty, using the two dogs he brought as puppies from Jerusalem, and at once we see that this is his calling: he knows all about the work, can tell when dogs sniff the taint of wolves in the air, and understands all about breeding and the quality of rams, and is a tender father to the lambs. He also shows himself to be a thoroughly practical man of affairs, organising the putting up of barriers against robbers, and, regretfully, seeing to the sale of the sheep to butchers.

This is the life needful to him in his pursuit of the knowledge of God:

> In the cenoby, he said, men do not think, they only read, but in the fields a shepherd need never lose sight of the thought that leads him. A good shepherd can think while watching his sheep; and as the flock was feeding in good order, he took up the thread of a thought to which he had become attached since his discovery that signs and sounds of God's presence are never lacking on earth. As God's constant companion and confidant he had come to comprehend that the world of nature was a manifestation of the God he knew in himself. I know myself, he said one day, but I do not know the God which is above, for he seems to be infinite; nor do I know nature, which is beyond me, for that, too, seems to run into an infinite that is not that of God. A few moments later it seemed to him he might look upon himself

as an islet between two infinities. But to which was he nearer in eternity? Ah, if he knew that! And it was then that a conviction fell upon him that if he remained on the hills he would be able to understand many things that were obscure to him to-day. It will take about two years, he said, and then many things that are dark will become clear. Two infinities, God and nature. It was just then that his eyes fell on a yoe wandering near some scrub. A wolf, he said, may be lurking there. I must bring her back; and he put a stone into his sling. A wolf is lurking there, he continued, else Gorbotha would not stand growling. Gorbotha, a golden-haired dog, like a wolf in build, stood snuffing the breeze, whilst Thema, his sister, sought her master's hand.[5]

When the dogs have done what is wanted of them, Jesus

resumed his meditation, saying to himself that if aching bones obliged him to return to the cenoby he would have to give up thinking. For one only thinks well in solitude and when one thinks for oneself alone; but in the cenoby the brethren think together. All the same my life on the hills is not over yet, and an hour later he put his pipe to his lips and led his flock to different hills, for, guided by some subtle sense, he seemed to divine the springing up of new grass; and the shepherds, knowing of this instinct for pasturage, were wont to follow him, and he was often at pains to elude them, for on no hillside is there grass enough for many flocks.[6]

Thus is the portrait of Jesus piece by piece built up, and again and again we are led to follow him in thought rather than in action. Finally there is a certain surprise. One night a stranger approaches the cenoby asking for admittance, and with much hesitation, lest he be a robber, the brethren let him in. He is a strange sight:

His large and bowed shoulders made his bald, egg-shaped skull (his turban had fallen in his flight) seem ridiculously small; it was bald to the ears, and a thick black beard spread over his face like a broom, and nearly to the eyes; thick black

[5] *Op. cit.*, pp. 344-5.
[6] *Op. cit.*, p. 345.

eyebrows shaded the eyes so piercing and brilliant that the
three Essenes were aware that a man of great energy had
come among them.[7]

This is Paul of Tarsus, who on his way from Jericho to Caesarea
has lost his companion Timothy, and has come for help and
shelter to the Essenes. Paul tells them his story, and how he is in
a sense a prisoner of the Romans because he stirs up trouble
among the Jews with a strange doctrine of Christ and Christianity.
He relates his vision on the road to Damascus, and of how Christ
spoke to him from Heaven.

Here again there is much discussion, especially about the
"strange doctrine" of resurrection, and whether it be of the body
or of the spirit only, including in a splendid passage the relation of
intellect to sense. Jesus, naturally, is much perturbed by all this,
and the mistaken notion of his own resurrection. He regards it as
largely his own fault, and is full of remorse for what he now
considers his unwarranted arrogance:

I should have remained an Essene shepherd following my
flocks in the hills, but John did well to come out of the
desert to preach the end of the world, for God had willed
him to preach it. His teaching was true when he was the
teacher, but when I became his disciple his teaching became
false; it turned me from my natural self into such great
harshness of mind that in Nazareth when my mother came
with my brothers and sisters to the synagogue, I said:
Woman, I have no need of thee; and when Joseph of
Arimathea returned to me after a long attendance by his
father's bedside (his father had lain in great sickness for
many months; it was through Joseph's care that he had been
saved from death, Joseph was a good son), I told him he
must learn to hate his father and his mother if he would
become worthy to follow me. But my passion was so great
in those days that I did not see that my teaching was not less
than blasphemy against God, for God has created the world
for us to live in it, and he has put love of parents into our
hearts because he wishes us to love our parents, and if he has
put into the heart of man love of woman, and into the heart

[7] *Op. cit.*, p. 371.

of woman love of man, it is because he wishes both to enjoy that love.

I fear to think of the things I said at that time, but I must speak of them. One man asked me before he left all things to follow me if he might not bury his father first. I answered: Leave the dead to bury their dead. . . . My teaching grew more and more violent. It is not peace I bring you, but a sword. . . . I said, too, that I came to divide the house; to set father against mother, brother against brother, sister against sister. . . . It was to repent of the evil seed I had sown that I returned to Kerith. . . . In the time I am telling I was so exalted by the many miracles which I had performed by the power of God or the power of a demon, I know not which, that I encouraged my disciples to speak of me as the son of David . . . pride lifted me above myself, and I went about asking who I was: Moses, Elijah, Jeremiah, or the Messiah promised to the Jews –[8]

on hearing which Paul cries out "A madman! A madman! or possessed by some evil spirit", and rushes out of the cenoby, thus missing the most moving part of Jesus' confession. Finally Jesus, out with his flock, finds Paul exhausted on his way to Caesarea, gives him water, and takes him to rejoin his lost companion.[9]

It has been necessary to give the skeletal outline of the affecting story to show what Moore was trying to convey. For though the main interest is in the conversations, the philosophies, and the search after God, the novelistic idea is not entirely absent, coming out most in the relations of Joseph and Dan. The latter wants his son to be a good business man – which in many ways he is – to marry and provide him with grandchildren. But Joseph is in no way a lover. Besides, he is unorthodox, and Dan fears his going to Jerusalem, lest there, on account of his differing from the Pharisees with their forms and observances (for he feels with Jesus that sacrifices and rites estrange men from God) he should be

---

[8] *Op. cit.*, pp. 432, 433.
[9] Moore's brief play *The Passing of the Essenes* (1931) gives a slightly different version. Jesus has been bound, not nailed, to the cross, and all the brethren of the cenoby except Jesus and two others accompany Paul on his proselytising journey.

stabbed to death by a Zealot, as he ultimately is. The two
chapters xiv and xv give an account of this affectionate tension.

The novelistic element is far stronger in *Héloïse and Abélard*.
We get an awakening view of the characters – Canon Fulbert,
Madelon, and a few others, besides those of the protagonists, and
are eager to follow the story. Though there are complexities,
fewer clouds arise out of clouds; nor are the unspoken monologues so dominating yet still important. There is the same
enchantment, almost the same compulsion to be involved in
generalised thinking. The prose, too, is much the same, giving
the sense of distance in time, here in the twelfth century, the main
philosophic theme, not insisted upon, being the relation between
faith and reason. At this point another long quotation may be
permitted. The escaping lovers are riding away

> . . . when an old Romanesque church, lying low, almost squat,
> served him for an illustration, and he made it plain to her that
> the round arch was superseded by the pointed; for it allowed
> the builders to build higher, to raise their roofs over a
> hundred feet, thereby inspiring the worshippers to lift their
> thoughts as well as their hearts Godward. The Romanesque
> church represents faith, he said, and the new church faith
> enforced with reason, a little exordium that filled Héloïse's
> eyes with wonder and her heart with reverence, though she
> would have wished to hear of faith and reason at some more
> suitable time, for at that moment the green streak of morning
> was passing away and rose-coloured clouds were beginning
> in the sky. A lovely day is preparing, she said, and the
> trouvère getting the better of the philosopher he forgot faith
> and reason, and said: The beauty of the larches is enough.
> But his apology was not to her taste, for she felt that any
> concession from him was out of keeping, and answered that
> it was reason, not faith, that helped men to an appreciation
> of the spring for itself. She put it to him, asking if it were
> not true that if we fail to turn to reason each springtide must
> seem like a separate act of God. Her words were pleasing to
> him. I will not deny that the words Faith and Reason exalt
> me, he answered, for they represent a battle that is in pro-
> gress between the Church and human nature, but I am afraid

that when I meet people they will say: ah, he will talk to us now about faith and reason, and instead of speaking about what is nearest my heart, I speak of other things, for though no one would believe it, I am at heart a shy man.[10]

The emotional theme of the book, as one would expect, is of the nature of love, which in itself can become a kind of mystic faith. There is a curious episode (Chapter XXII) where Abélard and Rodebœuf (of whom more later) meet a hermit, a sometime knight, old, but erect, full of vigour and health, who says of his love:

> Malberge is my soul, for nothing is essential in me except her. Without her I should not have been myself, and were she taken from me I should be nothing; therefore I say, and not without reason, it seems to me, that the Lady Malberge is my soul. Or my love of her is my soul, if your mood, sir, is to split hairs. But, said Abélard, the soul is all spirit. My love is all spirit, Gaucelm answered. Was your love then unfleshly? Abélard asked. By no means; it was in my lady's bed that I came to know myself. I was nothing before I entered it, merely a man given over to vain commerce with every woman that took his fancy. And you have never wavered from your love? Abélard inquired. Wavered from my love? You might as well ask if I have ever wavered from my senses. All I see and hear is my Lady Malberge. She is the bird that sings within me; she is the fruit that I taste – In memory, Abélard interposed. Memory is the truer reality, Gaucelm answered. She is the flower that I meet upon my way and that I gather, and for each flower that I gather another springs up in its place, the same flower sometimes or else a more beautiful flower than the one I have gathered....[11]

and he goes on to account how originally, with her sleeve on his arm, he irresistibly won a tourney.

The book opens amusingly enough with a picture of Canon Fulbert, who takes lightly his duties at Notre-Dame, but very

[10] *Héloïse and Abélard*, Ebury Edition, London (Heinemann) 1936 (reprint of final version, 1925) pp. 158-9.   [11] *Op. cit.*, p. 268.

seriously his creature comforts, being looked after by his in-
valuable Breton housekeeper Madelon, who is a superb cook. He
is fond of assemblies of his friends when cakes and wine are
relished, and lute-playing, but above all argument, which Madelon
is later to describe to Héloïse:

> And now I warn thee, talk of thy Virgil and thine Ovid, but
> let not the names of Roscelin and Champeaux or Abélard
> pass thy lips, for no sooner are those names mentioned than
> the place is like a rick of straw with somebody dropping
> lighted tinder about, for a word more or less will do it, and
> in a minute the fire will be jumping hither and thither,
> crackling, flaming, leaping; and if it doesn't blaze, smoking
> in sullen ill-humour, setting everybody coughing.[12]

The tenor of his life is upset by the death of his brother in the
First Crusade, so that he becomes the guardian of the latter's
widow Jeanne, and of his daughter Héloïse. Jeanne, however,
shortly afterwards dies, and Fulbert is horrified at the idea that
the child will have to come to his beautiful house in the rue des
Chantres. The happy solution occurs to him; he will send the girl
to the convent at Argenteuil, and to the scandal of Madelon – who
had suckled her – packs her off after only one night. After all,
might she not have a vocation? Would it be fair to let the vision
of worldly life disturb this leaning? The convent becomes her
home, where she is occasionally visited by Madelon, who takes
her cakes and fruit. Fulbert feels that he ought to go to Argenteuil, but then, mightn't this put wrong thoughts into her head?
The idea, for instance, of succeeding to his not despicable wealth?

After seven years he decides that he ought to invite her to his
house – just for three or four days: but Madelon insists upon six,
"and six evenings with a prattling girl seemed an unmerited
punishment". But when Héloïse arrives, Fulbert is charmed. She
likes his house, which she dimly remembers, finding the view
from the windows so beautiful that he takes her for a walk round
Paris, and is pleased to find how well she appreciates architecture.
What is more, he discovers that she is a first-rate Latinist, who can
help him to edit manuscripts. So she stays permanently, being
herself led to Ovid, Catullus, and especially Virgil, having hitherto

[12] *Op. cit.*, p. 51.

been confined to the religious writers. She is free to go where she will; and one day, instead of gathering bluebells on the banks of the Seine, she wanders, almost accidentally, into a lecture being given by Abélard, then at the height of his fame as a controversialist, held to be at least the equal of Plato and Aristotle. Héloïse is enraptured by his discourse, and when he issues out, throws herself at his feet and kisses his hand. A letter from him follows, to arrange a private meeting; soon we find him taking part in Fulbert's evening gatherings. When it is found that he would make an excellent tutor for Héloïse, and he declares his lodgings to be uncomfortable, Fulbert invites him to live with them.

The rest of the story is famous, and needs only the briefest recapitulation. The two fall in love, and when Fulbert discovers this, he sends Abélard back to his lodgings, where Héloïse visits him secretly. When in due course she becomes pregnant, the two, with Madelon, disguised as a monk and two nuns, make off on horseback to Britanny, to which they all three belong. There Abélard leaves her in charge of his married sister, goes back to Paris to lecture, and at once visits Fulbert, who is very angry at the whole affair, especially at the loss of Madelon, saying "Had Abélard left me Madelon I might have forgiven him the theft that love urged upon him". Abélard proposes to marry Héloïse, on condition that the marriage be kept secret. Fulbert agrees, insisting, however, that the compact shall be made before witnesses, but fails to keep the secret. Only one course is left the lovers: Héloïse goes back to the convent at Argenteuil and takes the veil, whereas Abélard resumes his teaching and becomes a monk. After a few years their son Astrolabe joins his mother, but she loses him, too, since he goes off on a child's Crusade and is never heard of again. For nine years she does not see Abélard, nor does he write. She hears that he has become a monk (not entered Holy Orders), and has been arraigned for heresy. At last she learns from Abélard the reason for all this. A few days after she had left for the convent, Fulbert had him seized and emasculated, so a career in the Church was not open to him. It is a sad, even a tragic story.

There is, however, some peace at the end. At one period Abélard had built himself a small mud and wattle hut on the banks of the Arduzon near Troyes, where he is joined by a number of disciples, each building his hut, and they lead what they regard as the life of the Essenes. Later the nuns at Argenteuil are dispossessed of their convent, and Abélard invites Héloïse with three other nuns to take over his huts. But he can never visit her "lest his enemies seeing him go thither, should mock and jeer, saying in their beards: the old wether still hankers after his yoe". Héloïse spends the rest of her life in passionate regret, writing her famous Letters to Abélard, now Abbot of St Gildas.

Moore tells the story superbly, creating a glowing aura by his hypnotic prose, making the characters emerge vividly. Fulbert and Madelon have already been touched on. Héloïse is more subtly brought out. Beautiful and very intelligent, she enjoys the loveliness of things, and is imaginatively warm-hearted, as we see when she delouses a bird struggling on the window-sill, or wishes, when wolves are being hunted through Paris, to let in one scratching for admittance at the door. Her feelings towards Abélard are divided. Though she loves him as a woman does a man, what she is desperately eager for is his fame, for she loves him as a great philosopher. Content to be his mistress, she does not want to marry him since this would make impossible his advancement in the Church, where she sees him as Archbishop, or even Pope. She herself has no strong religious leanings, and says very early, "I could never take any interest in religion"; and after Astrolabe disappears she loses her faith altogether; she had lived for nine years as a nun "with a lie in her heart always and often on her lips".

Abélard is a more striking because more complex character, torn by conflicting desires. The over-riding spring for his action is a passion for argument. A great philosopher, invincible in argument, rejoicing in dialectics (he had given over his estate in Britanny to pursue his teaching), being the inventor, one might say, of scholastic philosophy, he is also an outstanding musician and singer, a notable *trouvère* and gleeman, known in that field as Lucien de Marolle; he has serious thoughts of making his career as such. For all his love for Héloïse he does not share her ecclesiastical ambitions for him; the higher he rises the less freedom for argument he would have; as Pope he would be virtually tongue-tied. He has great pride in himself, and longs to humble all those who do not support his brand of Nominalism, believing that neither Realism nor Nominalism are altogether right, and would substitute Conceptualism. "I think thou art sorry, Héloïse, that I am so immodest a man", he says: "Time and again I have tried to check myself, to conform, but no man checks himself or even conforms, if he be a man." Yet his admiring sister says to him, "Humility is thy fault, Pierre".

There are certain other stories told, such as that of Gaucelm, already touched upon; that of Flamietta whose maidservant Matilda is really Gérard de Montador; and notably that of the Comte de Rodebœuf, whose career as a noble who has sacrificed all to be a *trouvère* weaves itself into the tale of the two lovers. Also we hear the story of Peronnik, the village fool who is not such a fool after all, originally told to Astrolabe in Breton by Madelon, and which Héloïse translates into French to teach her son the language. It is fairly fully recounted in three places, but in 1924 Moore developed it into a separate booklet, and added it to *Daphnis and Chloë*. It is interesting enough, and shares many of the characteristics of the major works, but is not of first importance.

Aphrodite in Aulis (1930) is not to be classed with the "epics", the manner in prose-writing is only an echo of that in the others. The interior monologues are not so deeply philosophic, nor are the main figures of dominating importance; physical rather than spiritual beauty is the theme. It is a pleasant success story. Kebren, son of an Athenian fishmonger, is a handsome young man, an ideal figure for a messenger in the drama: but not content with those parts, he becomes a rhapsodist, reading Homer to spell-bound audiences. A dream tells him to go to Aulis, whence the Greek fleet sailed for Troy. There he meets Otanes, a great ship-owner and trader, becomes his associate, and marries his daughter Biote. They have two sons, Rhesos, who becomes a distinguished sculptor praised by Phidias, and Thrasillos an architect; both are employed in completing the Parthenon. We just meet Phidias, Sophocles, Euripides, and the young Aristophanes.

The name of Aphrodite appears because they are going to build a temple at Aulis, and there is great, even violent controversy as to whether the presiding deity shall be Poseidon or Aphrodite. Rhesos wants to sculpt an Aphrodite, but cannot quite get the effect he aims at. He consults an oracle, a pythoness, who tells him to await the coming of the foam-born goddess by the sea. She fails to appear, but after many days he sees two girls swimming in. They, daughters of a rich sheep-farmer, have come to examine each others' bodies to decide which of them has the prettier rump. One of them, Earine, is exactly what Rhesos has been looking for as a model for the statue he has been unable to hew into shape: he marries her, and his brother takes the sister.

The whole might have been a trite enough story, but it is woven in the tapestry of Moore's later prose, and the characters emerge subtly enough. Kebren is a good solid business partner for Otanes, continues as a rhapsodist, and hankers after travel, absenting himself for two years in Egypt, studying the pyramids and the gods. He has his moods, as we find when we accompany him on a boar-hunt:

> From far and near the horns sounded, and a great boar, his sow beside him, came galloping down a glade, leading a long string of younglings only just off the dugs. Soon they will be surrounded, said Kebren, the old boar ripping up a hound or two before the hunters come up with their long spears. And so vivid was his foreseeing of the hounds rushing upon their quarry, tearing and snarling and being tossed hither and thither, that he forgot his horse, and the animal grazed, Kebren sitting like a stock upon him. At last the forest was silenced, and his thoughts too were hushed. Nothing remained but a sense of his unhappiness, an unhappiness from which he could not escape, having root in the very substance of his being and more than once on his way home he muttered: An unhappiness which may one day press me to my own destruction.[13]

The whole story is, even more than the previous ones, dotted, one might say, with incidents. There is, for example, the one of the wolf, Ajax, which, unlike those in the other books, and most of those here, is a tame one, having been separated from his pack, and is looked after by Rhesos, who one day takes his mother to see him. They talk of various things as they go, and then:

[13] *Aphrodite in Aulis*, London (Heinemann) 1937 (reprint of final version, 1932) pp. 98-9.

But here we are. Biote asked him why he spoke in an under-
tone, and he answered that if he raised his voice Ajax, who
was doubtless in his den asleep, would awaken. And I'd
have thee see him first. To rush out upon me? Rushing out
is only his play, mother; there is no danger. But, Rhesos,
thou wouldst not have me go in alone! And then from
vanity or to prove her courage to him, she said: I will go in
alone since thou tellest me I shall not be torn or bitten or
roughly treated. Rhesos raised his voice, and the wolf with
ears erect came forth to see his master. Rhesos cried to him
two or three times, and every time Ajax stopped and laid
back his ears. The animal's delight was plain and encouraged
by it Rhesos opened the door and let his mother into the
garden. The wolf rushed forward and Biote screamed, but
Ajax gained some knowledge of his visitor even as he raced,
and raising himself on his hind-legs he put his paws round
Biote's neck and licked her sweetly.[14]

The characters throughout the book are deftly, if not very profoundly drawn, as are those in *The Brook Kerith* or *Héloïse and Abélard*: but then that is not the object of the presentation.

On the other hand there are many observations that strike the
reader, as much from the picturesqueness of the imaging as from
the depth of the thought. Otanes is caught by a phrase his wife
uses while embroidering: "To complete the design of the Gods
we have to put a stitch here and there." A little later conversing
with his son-in-law he remembers it, consciously or not, and
remarks: "I like to listen to thee, Kebren, for listening to thee
brings back my youth. And they talked on, returning every now
and then to the baffling, unanswerable question whether all is
blind chance – or stitches, Otanes interjected, in some great
design that the Fates are weaving behind the Gods." Or again
there is a longer passage where Otanes, having been very ill,
ruminates with Kebren about death:

Religions arise, we know not whence nor how; they are bred
like the mayflies among the reeds; they rise from the depths
of the waters. Priests hold out their hands and say: We will
interpret the mystery of life; we will lead you, and there shall

[14] *Op. cit.*, pp. 110-11.

be no death; and steeped in fables men forget they must die. All our lives we are weaving fables or drawing veils around us. The most beautiful passages in our poets are evocations to death, for death, or perhaps I should say the fear of death, is everything to man ... the Gods or the Fate over and above the Gods implanted in man the fear of death, for without it we should be as animals, living in quiet ignorance and dying in the same.... It is the fear of death that separates us from the animals, whether for good or for evil I know not.[15]

Later, Kebren and Rhesos are once more talking, this time during a boar-hunt, and Rhesos is "wondering of what his father was thinking".

Thinking of the Parthenon? of Phidias? of Ajax? he inquired. If I was thinking of anything, Kebren replied, it was of the leaves showering about us, without knowledge of their destination, like ourselves; and the remark seeming to Rhesos trite and old-fashioned, he laughed. Laughing at thine old father's philosophy, Kebren said good-humouredly. Is it not true, Rhesos, that we are as casual as the leaves? But thou'rt too young to philosophise. Still, thou hast thoughts, for to be mortal is to think.[16]

When at a certain time Kebren is away, Biote and Otanes discuss him, his sense at having failed himself as a rhapsodist, an artist, being too much taken up with the world. Biote says:

Were he to return and take me in his arms, saying: I have failed as a rhapsodist, I would console him with my love and with stories of his children. Biote, thou dost expect too much. A man's ideas are dearer to him than wife or children, for they are his soul, and no man will confess his soul to be base and worthless, not even to himself.[17]

Otanes is the great philosopher of the tale, loving to discourse with his grandsons, a little platitudinously, it may seem to us, but always with metaphorical speech. He answers the question put to him by Thrasillos, "But are not the Gods immortal?"

[15] *Op. cit.*, p. 67.   [16] *Op. cit.*, p. 97.   [17] *Op. cit.*, p. 125.

We appeal to the Gods in our afflictions and troubles, Otanes answered, and these having seemingly passed over like the clouds, we make mockery of the Gods. Is there no God in which we may believe always, grandfather? Yes, grandson – Providence! On looking back everybody believes himself to have been led by the hand. A sad belief, said Thrasillos. Why sad? Otanes asked, for in it we find escape from our dread that we and all the world are no more than blind chance. Go on talking, grandfather; I like to listen, for thou art wise. Not in myself, Otanes answered; mine is but the wisdom of years. Our minds enlarge like rivers as they approach the sea.[18]

Soon Thrasillos discusses this with Rhesos, and it would seem that the philosophy that guided Otanes was that each man should pursue his art. He is also something of an epigrammatist: "From the beginning a man's life is like an arrow, barbed and feathered. It springs from the bow on its fated journey, to fall short, to fly too high or too low. At last a well-directed arrow reaches the mark, and the Archer laughs, for the quarry is but a shadow."

No one will deny that these final works are outstanding; in the quality of the imagination which can so vividly resurrect past ages, causing us to live in those times, sharing the outlook and the thoughts of the people then having their being, seeing things as they see them. Much is due to the interweaving, tapestry-like nature of the prose, which, with its long sentences, carries us over the whole picture, and more, into the scene, so that like Kebren when thinking of his future "as quietly as an otter slides into the water he returned to the dream that lay ahead of him", we slide into the dream that Moore offers us.

How much is owing to the carefully invented style may be assessed by comparing any of the passages quoted above with, say, this one from *The Untilled Field* (1903):

No one had ever addressed Biddy as Madam before, and, very pleased, she wiped the table clean so that she could spread the designs upon it, and the first he showed her were the four Evangelists, but he said he would like a woman's present to the church to be in a somewhat lighter style, and

18 *Op. cit.*, pp. 139-40.

produced a picture of St. Cecilia. As Biddy seemed doubtful, he suggested a group of figures would look handsomer than a single figure. She was fascinated by what she saw, but unable to put aside the idea of the window that had grown up in her mind, she began her relation.[19]

Or this from *Ave*, the first volume of his autobiography, which, later than the novel, being published in 1911, more nearly approaches the final works in manner:

> The slight success that has attended my writings did not surprise my relations as much as it surprised me, and what seems curious is that, if the success had been twice what it was, it would not have restored the confidence in myself that I lost in childhood. I am always a novice, publishing his first book, wondering if it is the worst thing ever written; and I am as timid in life as in literature. It is always difficult for me to believe that my friends are glad to see me. I am never quite sure that I am not a bore – an unpleasant belief, no doubt, but a beneficial one, for it saves me from many blunders, and I owe to it many pleasant surprises: that day at Steer's, when Tonks interrupted me in one of my usual disquisitions on art with – Isn't it nice to have him among us again criticising our paintings? [Moore seems to have missed the possible irony in this] I had come back from Ireland after an absence of two years, and I shall never forget the delicious emotion that his words caused me. I had never suspected my friends would miss me, or that it would mean so much to them to have me back again.[20]

He develops this with an irrelevant reference to Rousseau.

The ideas in the later works are intricately interwoven; and if we apply to Moore what Héloïse said to Fulbert about Virgil, try to analyse the style, notice the "clouds arising out of clouds", and sense the melodious voice that brings out sentence after sentence, like silk from a spool, some light may come. It is evident that this description does not apply to the earlier work, because there Moore does not allow his mind to wander, though the auto-

[19] *The Untilled Field*, London (Fisher Unwin) 1903, p. 118.
[20] *Ave*, London (Heinemann) 1947, pp. 62-3.

biography is a link. The sentences now are longer, though short ones are not absent, while a paragraph may run over two pages. Whereas in earlier books a paragraph has a definite subject, and is shaped with a beginning, middle and end, in later ones our minds too wander, make explorations, a paragraph possibly containing a deal of varied matter. But always the vowel sounds are carefully modulated, and provide the music essential to prose that moves the imagination.

It is this language unwinding itself phrase after sustained phrase, rather than "thou" and "hath" and so on, that gives these final works their distance in time, their remoteness from present-day actuality, which the dates of the stories demand. It is suitable for the mundane or matter-of-fact, the splendid description, or the philosophic aphorism, and, moreover, binds together the complexity of the story, or, rather, stories. The danger is that its very perfection may become soporific, lulling the reader to inattention, or to neglecting the event to watch the unwinding of the spool, or to follow the movements of the clouds.

Brendan Kennelly

GEORGE MOORE'S LONELY VOICES: A STUDY OF HIS SHORT STORIES

I

In his introduction to *Celibate Lives*, George Moore has an imaginary conversation in which, with a characteristically light touch, he reveals something of his attitude to the short story. When his imaginary protagonist asks Moore if he is for or against adventures, he replies that he does not deal in adventures "but in soul cries".[1] Here, Moore gets to the very core of what has preoccupied Irish short story writers ever since his time – the problem of man's loneliness. Frank O'Connor, in his extremely perceptive study of the short story, *The Lonely Voice*, writes: "There is in the short story at its most characteristic something we do not often find in the novel – an intense awareness of human loneliness. Indeed, it might be truer to say that while we often read a familiar novel again for companionship, we approach the short story in a very different mood. It is more akin to the mood of Pascal's saying: "le silence éternel des ces espaces infinis m'effraie."[2] It is not unfair to say that George Moore gave Irish short story writers that theme of human loneliness which has so fascinated their imagination. It is in every story of *Dubliners*, and that remarkable collection ends with a lyrical affirmation of the fact that man is essentially alone. Joyce, in fact, takes Gabriel Conroy to the very threshold of the loneliness that is unspeakable – the loneliness of death.

His soul had approached that region where dwell the vast

[1] *Celibate Lives*, Ebury Edition, London (Heinemann) 1937, p. viii.
[2] *The Lonely Voice*, London (Macmillan) 1963, p. 19.

hosts of the dead. He was conscious of, but could not apprehend, their wayward and flickering existence. His own identity was fading out into a grey impalpable world: the solid world itself, which these dead had one time reared and lived in, was dissolving and dwindling.[3]

Frank O'Connor, Seán O'Faoláin, Liam O'Flaherty, Mary Lavin, and Benedict Kiely continually and skilfully explore the dark pit of loneliness. The same preoccupation is evident in the work of more recent writers such as Edna O'Brien, James Plunkett, and John McGahern. The fact that several of these writers frequently examine this problem in comic terms is a measure of their skill – laughter is seen as the sunny emphasis of a desolate fact. Moore is, of course, a fine comic writer, and it was Moore who first pointed out to modern Irish writers the fact that the best short stories consist of brief but profound and luminous insights into the lives of those who haunt the fringes of society, drab figures who live anonymously and suffer quietly. I would like to examine *Celibate Lives*, *The Untilled Field*, and *A Story-Teller's Holiday* in an effort to show the various ways in which Moore examined the problem of loneliness; how he found a form that later Irish writers tried to perfect; I shall try also to evaluate his importance in the distinguished tradition of the Irish short story.

Celibate Lives would have been more accurately entitled *Lonely Lives* because in this collection of stories one is struck not so much by the celibacy of any of the characters, but by the loneliness that is their typical condition. The five stories in the volume have for titles the proper names of the main characters concerned, and Moore subjects each of these people to a penetrating and sustained scrutiny. The opening story, "Wilfrid Holmes", concerns a typically casual outcast, the "fool" of the Holmes family, the one who refuses to work, and therefore mars the respectability which his relatives esteem so much. Wilfrid is a childlike figure who, in his timid and harmless way, plays at being scholar, musician, composer, and journalist, living all the time on a small allowance from his aunt. The crisis in his life comes when the allowance fails to arrive, and he experiences that moment of bitter self-awareness, of implacable self confrontation, which so many of

[3] *Dubliners*, Harmondsworth (Penguin) 1962, p. 220.

Joyce's characters also experience in *Dubliners*. Wilfrid sees himself for the outcast he is. He understands that he cannot understand, and that he cannot be understood.

> Nobody would understand that he could not earn his living. Nobody had ever understood this except his mother, and nobody ever would. He laid no blame on anybody; he did not understand it himself. . . . But he could not earn his living, and, worst of all, he could not tell why. . . . Nobody would understand – he did not understand. A frightened look came into his face, for he saw in that instant a lonely figure, a confessed failure, amid sad shrubberies and dismal woods.[4]

In Joyce's finest short story, "The Dead", Gabriel Conroy experiences a similar moment of harrowing self-vision.

> He saw himself as a ludicrous figure, acting as a penny-boy for his aunts, a nervous, well-meaning sentimentalist, orating to vulgarians and idealizing his own clownish lusts, the pitiable fatuous fellow he had caught a glimpse of in the mirror.[5]

In both Moore and Joyce, one of the chief effects of a fully realised loneliness is the brutal moment of self-knowledge that is merciless and complete. Though Moore's story ends on a comparatively happy note, we have seen Wilfrid Holmes stripped bare as a tree in winter down to his essential timidity and mediocrity, a black sheep without talent or resource, a devoted nonentity, a pariah committed to a life of quiet absurdity.

The loneliness of "Priscilla and Emily Lofft" is that of a woman who has lost her sister. Emily had known Priscilla so intimately that "Priscilla had never seemed another being to her, but her second self, her shadow, her ghost, each akin to the other as the sound and its echo".[6] Alone in the house after Priscilla's death, Emily realises her loneliness:

> . . . sitting on the little rep sofa, her eyes brimming with occasional tears, she bethought herself of the life that awaited her without Priscilla, alone in the world, without

---

[4] *Celibate Lives*, pp. 13-14.   [5] *Dubliners*, pp. 216-17.
[6] *Celibate Lives*, p. 29.

parents or relations. Aunt Clara was gone; a few distant cousins there were, dispersed over the world; a few neighbours, a few friends, scattered through Dublin; but nobody whom she could love. Lonely evenings . . .[7]

Out of Emily's loneliness springs her responsibility to the dead Priscilla. Priscilla had died trying to tell something to Emily, and had managed to write the words "in the garden" before she expired. Later, in the garden, Emily discovers a French novel which Priscilla had been reading – the story of an unfaithful wife with two lovers. This was the closest Priscilla had ever come to an emotional experience. Following her dying wishes, Emily destroys the book, and having fulfilled her responsibility to the dead, is thereafter, as it were, free to be lonely among the living.

> . . . she was free to leave this dusty old house and the dusty conventions in which half her life had been spent. She was free to return to Aix and to live like other English spinsters on a small income, travelling whither she listed, from one boarding-house to another, seeking – Does anybody do more than to seek and to find, mayhap, something?[8]

An important aspect of Moore's genius is that he continually sees loneliness as an integral part of ordinary life. An Irish poet, Patrick Kavanagh, speaks in his long poem, *The Great Hunger*, about "the weak, washy way of true tragedy",[9] and goes on to portray the wretchedness of the humdrum life of his central character, Patrick Maguire. In Moore's stories, one finds a similar kind of perception. One of his most agonising pictures of loneliness is his story of Albert Nobbs, a waiter in a Dublin hotel, a woman who, in order to survive during her youth, dressed as a man and so managed to make a living. With a very daring stroke, Moore creates a situation in which Albert's secret is revealed to another woman, also disguised as a man. This other person, Hubert Page, explains that she found happiness by leaving her brutal husband and her children and by setting up house with a girl. She thus plants in Albert's mind the possibility of a similar solution to her problem. Page agrees to keep Albert's secret, and

---

[7] *Op. cit.*, pp. 32-3.   [8] *Op. cit.*, pp. 42-3.
[9] Patrick Kavanagh, *Collected Poems*, London (MacGibbon & Kee) 1964, p. 53.

leaves. Albert dreams of happiness and becomes involved in a farcical courtship with a girl, Helen Dawes, a colourful, vulgar girl who ruthlessly exploits Albert, while she has an affair with a scullion in the hotel. The courtship ends ludicrously and for a while Albert is heart-broken. She recovers her spirits somewhat, but then becomes ill and dies. Her secret is an open book to the ready mockers of Dublin. Page, the other disguised woman, returns, and hearing of Albert's death, decides to go home to the husband and children she had abandoned fifteen years previously.

Moore handles here a theme which, in the hands of a less skilled writer, could easily degenerate into a burlesque of incredible disguise and sensational disclosure. Think of it! Two women disguised as men find themselves in the same bed, and when one of them is bitten by a very persistent flea, the secret is out! But Moore completely avoids the attractive comic distortions of caricature, and instead describes, with wonderfully compassionate insight, Albert Nobbs's daily indignities, the small revolting brutalities of an insensitive world, and above all, the constant loneliness of the "perhapser", Moore's name for Albert Nobbs, who could hardly claim to be either man or woman. Albert's life had been

> ... a mere drifting, it seemed to her, from one hotel to another, without friends; meeting, it is true, sometimes men and women who seemed willing to be friendly. But her secret forced her to live apart from men as well as women; the clothes she wore smothered the woman in her; she no longer thought and felt as she used to when she wore petticoats, and she didn't think and feel like a man though she wore trousers. What was she? Nothing, neither man nor woman, so small wonder she was lonely.[10]

An outcast from both sexes, Albert fails miserably with the girl, Helen Dawes. In despair, she walks the streets of Dublin, finally picking up a street-walker. But she fails even with the street-walker, who simply walks off with a friend. This is the depth of Albert's desolation and it is very movingly described by Moore. Albert's being is a chaos of grief.

The street-walkers have friends, and when they meet them

[10] *Celibate Lives*, p. 64.

their troubles are over for the night; but my chances have gone by me; and, checking herself in the midst of the irrelevant question, whether it were better to be casual, as they were, or to have a husband that you could not get rid of, she plunged into her own grief, and walked sobbing through street after street, taking no heed of where she was going.[11]

Humbert Wolfe says that "George Moore has the widest human sympathy of any English novelist".[12] An extravagant claim, surely, yet when one considers the compassionate accuracy with which Moore traces the pathetic course of Albert Nobbs's life through its long years of deprivation and failure, right up to the last, lonely moments, portrayed in precisely the right kind of intense understatement, one can at least appreciate, if not wholly agree with, Wolfe's enthusiastic judgment. A brilliant structural device was Moore's decision *not* to end the story at that point when Albert dies, but to bring back the other disguised woman, Hubert Page, who, seeing the circumstances of Albert's death, decides to return to her own abandoned family. Page's desire to finally choose that domestic stability for which Albert so long and vainly yearned merely emphasises the pity of Albert's death – an essentially lost creature whose life began in bastardy and ended in anonymity.

Moore understood that loneliness manifests itself in several ways. In the case of Wilfrid Holmes, it appeared as childish eccentricity; with Emily Lofft, it meant an almost visionary awareness of her dead sister and a final resolution to leave the house where they had lived together; and it involved Albert Nobbs in what turned out to be an absurd quest for happiness. In the longest story in *Celibate Lives*, entitled "Henrietta Marr", Moore examines what is best described as the predatory energy of loneliness. Etta Marr is a woman with whom several men fall in love, who is attracted to men, but who is unable to give herself sexually. Her dilemma makes her attractive and treacherous, lovable and phoney. Moore traces her career through five relationships, skilfully drawing a deepening sense of Etta's brilliant

---

[11] *Op. cit.*, p. 85.
[12] Humbert Wolfe, *George Moore*, Modern Writers Series, London (Butterworth) 1931, p. 125.

superficiality. Her inability to give herself makes her a patient, resolute flirt with a desire to have power over men. Once she acquires the power, however, she runs away from the possibility of any lasting attachment, so that she becomes a kind of professional hit-and-run lover, eager for triumph, afraid of the prize, yet always compelled to re-commence her conquest. In the end, she is rejected by the man she seems to want to marry, and kills herself.

Moore once wrote that "in the midst of our deepest emotions, we are acting a comedy with ourselves".[13] Etta Marr's basic inability to give herself involves her in a black comedy of loneliness. Her first lover is an English painter, Ralph Hoskin, who actually dies of a broken heart. Etta knows this, yet later, she tells another lover, Morton Mitchell, that Ralph had been slowly poisoned by his mistress whom Etta very much disliked. Moore, with his gift for understatement, merely hints at Etta's private fantasies of self-justification, and simply allows other characters in the story to suggest very briefly that Etta may be somewhat unbalanced, mentally. Further, she turns her fear to advantage, so that her sexual coldness becomes a demonstrable virtue, and her own personal deficiency an agent of her control over others. Moore is saying, I believe, that beauty that is lonely for Etta's reason is necessarily predatory and false. Etta is the essentially passionless woman who cannot fail to inspire passion in others, the fraud who attracts what is most genuine in men. This is not to say that her lovers are not aware of her falsehood. Morton Mitchell, her third lover, sees through Etta when she is at her most beautiful, during a ball given by the Comte de Malmédy.

> . . . as Etta went upstairs, three or four steps in front of the Comte, Morton saw her so clearly that the thought struck him that he had never seen her before. She appeared in that instant as a toy, a trivial toy made of coloured glass, and he wondered why he had been attracted by this bit of coloured glass.
>
> He laughed at his folly and went home, certain that he could lose her without pain . . .[14]

Morton, of course, is wrong, and falsehood continues to

---

[13] *Celibate Lives*, p. 37.   [14] *Op. cit.*, p. 160.

fascinate him until, and after, Etta leaves him for the Comte. At the end, when Etta is using her charms on an English clergyman, the Comte rejects her. When I said that Moore sees loneliness as predatory, I meant that it cuts both ways. Etta's rejection of Hoskin and Mitchell led to the death of one man and the unhappiness of the other; the Comte's rejection of Etta is directly responsible for her sudden death. In a bitterly ironic way, Etta, at the end, changes places with her first lover who, losing her, lost the will to live. Moore's story of this mutual ravaging process is told with admirable subtlety and deliberation. Albert Nobbs had dreamed of companionship and could not achieve it; Etta Marr is several times offered companionship but will not accept it, and when she requests it, she is refused. Because of the cruel ironies of her life and death, she is one of the loneliest of George Moore's lonely voices.

All the main characters in *Celibate Lives* opt out of the bustle of daily life in one way or another, and Moore, in a subtle but adamant way, repeats that sexual inadequacy is one of the truest sources of loneliness. Moore makes this point, not in an overt or brutal manner as certain modern novelists do, but through gradual implication, thereby creating a profound and far-reaching sense of the human complexity of the problem. In the final story, "Sarah Gwynn", we meet a young woman who retires to a convent to spend her life in prayer for the prostitute who helped her when she was in dire need. Again, Moore is here treating a theme which would have been a disaster in the hands of a less sophisticated writer, but just as he avoided burlesque in "Albert Nobbs", so does he escape sentimentality in "Sarah Gwynn".

Sarah is "a tiny, thread-paper girl in a straw hat, an alpaca jacket, and a thin skirt that did not hide her broken boots, a starveling",[15] a parlourmaid in the service of Dr O'Reardon. Very soon, she proves herself a paragon of efficiency, "the parlourmaid that every doctor desires and never finds",[16] but after a year of diligent and careful service, she informs the doctor that she is leaving because, she says, the gardener wants to marry her. O'Reardon presses her for further explanation, and Sarah tells him the story of her life; how after she had left her home in the North of Ireland to run away to Dublin, she almost starved but

---

[15] *Op. cit.*, pp. 178-9.   [16] *Op. cit.*, p. 183.

for the kindness of Phyllis Hoey, a factory-worker by day and a prostitute at night. Phyllis had asked Sarah to go on the streets with her, but Sarah, with help from Phyllis, had gone instead to a convent in Wales which she left after a few years to return to Dublin, go into the service of Doctor O'Reardon, and resume her search for Phyllis. The story ends with Sarah's decision to enter another convent where she can pray for the woman who had been kind to her.

Moore's insight into the mind of the self-effacing and distant Sarah is extremely penetrating. When Sarah takes up the narrative, going into a long monologue about her own life, we see deeply into a person whose hardship is equalled only by her courage. Moore had a gift fairly rare among short story writers and novelists – he could create totally authentic female characters. Esther Waters is his finest achievement in this respect, but Sarah Gwynn is also a triumphant creation. Moore puts in her mouth a completely appropriate language. Speaking of Phyllis's suggestion that she become a whore, she says,

> Phyllis didn't try to persuade me; she said that every girl must do the best she can for herself. She had often heard of girls marrying in the end off the streets, but she didn't want to say a word that might lead me where I didn't want to go. She said she quite understood, but there wouldn't be enough money for both of us if I didn't go, and in the end I might have been pushed into it, for I'm no better than Phyllis; and there never was a kinder soul, and maybe it's kindness that counts in the end.[17]

"Sarah Gwynn" is a moving conclusion to a moving book. Her calm, resolute withdrawal from life follows a pattern typical also of the other main characters. *Celibate Lives* proves that loneliness always has its origin in the heart but can lead practically anywhere; "Sarah Gwynn" shows that it can sometimes lead to a kind of peace.

2

Whatever loneliness and deprivation are in *The Untilled Field* are attributed by Moore to the stultifying influence of the Roman

[17] *Op. cit.*, p. 192.

Catholic Church in Ireland. Irish writers from Moore to Edna O'Brien have noted this and have very scrupulously and insistently pointed it out. Behind Irish puritanism and repression stretches a long, dark history of methodical English tyranny and futile Irish protest that helps to account for the emotional and moral climate of *The Untilled Field*. This collection of short stories is essentially a scrutiny of spiritual inertia just as *Dubliners* is an exposition of various kinds of paralysis. In the penultimate story, "The Wild Goose", Moore very succinctly describes how, in Ireland, inspiration degenerated into stagnation and passionate Christianity became pious inhibition. He speaks through the mouth of Ned Carmady whose political ambitions for Ireland have been thwarted by a puritanical wife and a meddling priest.

> For two centuries little else existed but Christ in Ireland; Ireland breathed Christ, saw and heard Christ during the fifth and sixth centuries. Christ was everywhere – above, beneath, within and without – Patrick's own words ... Ireland dozed long centuries in the happy aspiration of Christ, the living God, till suddenly God, remembering that happiness could not be allowed to last for ever, sent the Danes up the estuaries and rivers to burn and to pillage. And then, as if God's heart had softened, Brian Boru came and defeated the Danes. God, indeed, seemed to have wished to do something with Ireland in the tenth century, for the Cross of Cong, the Tara brooch, and Cormac's chapel are works of art; but he changed his mind, and ever since Ireland sinks deeper, struggling all the while to free herself, but held back by the parish priest; were another Saint Patrick to appear she would not listen.[18]

The lamentable change in Christianity from an inspired love of creation to a resolute distrust of life is the central theme of *The Untilled Field*. Other pathetic features follow from this: the atmosphere of unrelieved poverty and squalor; the frustration of all ideals; the suppression of individual thinking; the hysterical fear of sex as the supreme evil of which man is capable; the confusion of servility with obedience, furtive inhibition with virtuous

[18] *The Untilled Field*, Ebury Edition, London (Heinemann) 1937 (reprint of final version, 1931) pp. 217-18.

self-denial, caution with wisdom; the fear of full expression and hence the distrust of the artist – all these things are examined by Moore with considerable skill and subtlety. Co-existing with this theme of stagnation is the theme of escape – especially to America, the land of promise where it seems possible to fulfil these aspirations so tragically stifled in Ireland. In "Home Sickness", Moore not only points out how unquestioned clerical authority throttles all genuine vitality, but also effectively contrasts Irish sluggishness with American competence. Ironically, James Bryden returns from America to recover his health, falls in love with Margaret Dirken, but is horrified to find everybody pathetically submissive to the power of the priest:

> . . . he listened in mixed anger and wonderment to the priest, who was scolding his parishioners, speaking to them by name, saying that he had heard there was dancing going on in their homes. Worse than that, he said he had seen boys and girls loitering about the road, and the talk that went on was of one kind – love. He said that newspapers containing love stories were finding their way into the people's houses, stories about love, in which there was nothing elevating or ennobling. The people listened, accepting the priest's opinion without question. And their pathetic submission was the submission of a primitive people clinging to religious authority, and Bryden contrasted the weakness and incompetence of the people about him with the modern restlessness and cold energy of the people he left behind.[19]

Because of this claustrophobic world with the priest at its centre, Bryden leaves Ireland and Margaret Dirken behind him, deliberately choosing the noisy bar-room in the Bowery slum to the intolerable repression of the Irish village. But, like all the chief characters in *Celibate Lives*, Bryden is an essentially lonely man, his loneliness deriving from his inability to forget the life he was compelled to reject. In the end, the rejected world becomes more real than the chosen one.

> There is an unchanging, silent life within every man that none knows but himself, and his unchanging silent life was

[19] *Op. cit.*, p. 34.

his memory of Margaret Dirken. The bar-room was forgotten and all that concerned it, and the things he saw most
clearly were the green hillside, and the bog lake and the rushes
about it, and the greater lake in the distance, and behind it the
blue line of wandering hills.[20]

If Moore had insisted that every Irish priest was despotic and
narrow-minded, his stories would have degenerated into sledge-
hammer polemic. But he is careful to set one priest's generosity
against another's meanness, one's tolerance against another's
inhumanity. In "Patchwork", there is a calm but effective contrast between an old priest's warmth and a young one's repressive
pettiness. Moore is here examining a national dilemma from
within, and fairly presenting both sides of the story. The only
trouble is, one feels, that the views of the young priest will
prevail.

> "Pleasure," said Father Tom. "Drinking and dancing,
> hugging and kissing each other about the lanes."
> "You said dancing – now, I can see no harm in it."
> "There's no harm in dancing, but it leads to harm. If they
> only went back with their parents after the dance, but they
> linger in the lanes."
> "It was raining the other night, and I felt sorry, and I said,
> 'Well, the boys and girls will have to stop at home to-night,
> there will be no courting to-night.' If you don't let them
> walk about the lanes and make their own marriages, they
> marry for money. These walks at eventide represent all the
> aspiration that may come into their lives. After they get
> married, the work of the world grinds all the poetry out of
> them."
> "Walking under the moon," said Father Tom, "with
> their arms round one another's waist, sitting for hours saying
> stupid things to each other – that isn't my idea of poetry.
> The Irish find poetry in other things than sex."
> "Mankind," said Father John, "is the same all the world
> over. The Irish aren't different from other races; do not
> think it. Woman represents all the poetry that the ordinary
> man is capable of appreciating."[21]

[20] *Op. cit.*, p. 39.   [21] *Op. cit.*, p. 62.

Consistently, throughout *The Untilled Field*, there is this balance between tyranny and tolerance, brutality and benevolence. One of Moore's most sympathetically-drawn characters is old Father Mac Turnan who, fearing for the future of Catholicism, writes a letter to the Pope in which he requests that the law of priestly celibacy be abolished. In this way, he calculates that all the priests of Ireland could become the fathers of thousands of Catholics, thereby ensuring the stability of that religion. Moore creates a strong picture of the old priest's naïveté and simple goodness and, during an interview with his Bishop concerning the letter to Rome, we are made aware of Mac Turnan's essential, customary loneliness, hidden under his concern for his poor parishioners.

> "A car will take you back, Father Mac Turnan. I will see to that. I must have some exact information about your poor people. We must do something for them."
>
> Father Mac Turnan and the Bishop were talking together when the car came to take Father Mac Turnan home, and the Bishop said:
>
> "Father Mac Turnan, you have borne the loneliness of your parish a long while."
>
> "Loneliness is only a matter of habit. I think, your Grace, I'm better suited to the place than I am for any other."[22]

Mac Turnan is a lonely dreamer with the compassionate aim of helping the poor people of his parish. He has the impractical but magnificent idea of building a little theatre in his western wilderness – a play-house in the waste. All his hopes centre on the extraordinary venture which, of course, fails – failure is Mac Turnan's daily bread. The local peasantry appreciate both his generous character and his odd ambition.

> "It was indeed, sir, a quare idea, but you see he's a quare man. He has been always thinking of something to do good, and it is said that he thinks too much. Father James is a very quare man, your honour."[23]

But the dominant impression left by Moore's priests is one of pious brutality. They insist not merely on guiding the people, but on completely ruling their lives. So they cajole, demote,

---

[22] *Op. cit.*, p. 116.   [23] *Op. cit.*, p. 129.

bully, arrange marriages, orate from the pulpit, control all social events, and manipulate private destinies according to their own will. To resist this will is to be expelled from society, and the individual who shows courage becomes an outcast branded with shame. Julia Cahill, in "Julia Cahill's Curse", an extremely beautiful girl with a mind of her own, refuses to allow the priest, Father Madden, to arrange her marriage with a farmer. As a result, the priest expels her from society and, in the end, she is compelled to go to America, but not before she puts a curse on the people. As a result, the little society becomes "the loneliest parish in Ireland".[24] The narrator of the story, looking at the land cursed by this outcast Venus, describes its peculiar desolation. Julia Cahill's loneliness, caused by the priest who hated her individuality, is the source of the loneliness afflicting the land. The priest's expulsion of beauty has impoverished the very soil of Ireland.

> . . . I noticed that though the land was good, there seemed to be few people on it, and what was more significant than the untilled fields were the ruins, for they were not the cold ruins of twenty, or thirty, or forty years ago when the people were evicted and their tillage turned into pasture – the ruins I saw were the ruins of cabins that had been lately abandoned . . .[25]

It is precisely this point that Moore drives home again and again – the priestly determination to smother or expel any manifestation of the individual dissenting will. There are two other outstanding examples towards the end of the book – one concerning a politician, the other an artist. Ned Carmady, in "The Wild Goose", an Irish-American with little interest in religion apart from his belief in the corruption of most of its practitioners, thinks that he is the man that Ireland needs and, initially encouraged by his wife, plunges into politics, but falls into disfavour as soon as it is recognised that he is anti-clerical, and that he desires a new spiritual and political order in Ireland. His wife is Ellen Cronin, a puritan who dreams of heroism and shuns reality. As his marriage grows thinner, the priest applies pressure, and Carmady, knowing that all his political hopes are now as dead as his marriage is cold, hoists his sail and leaves, like

[24] *Op. cit.*, p. 135.   [25] *Ibid.*

one of the "wild geese" – Irish soldiers who fled the country after the siege of Limerick in the seventeenth century. With Moore, exile is the recognition of failure in Ireland as well as the possibility of achievement elsewhere, and Carmady's departure is as much a desire for freedom as it is a gesture of disgust.

> ... he did not feel he was a free soul until the outlines of Howth began to melt into the grey drift of evening. There was a little mist on the water, and he stood watching the waves tossing in the mist, thinking it were well done that he had left home. If he had stayed he would have come to accept all the base moral coinage in circulation; and he stood watching the green waves tossing in the mist, at one moment ashamed of what he had done, at the next overjoyed that he had done it.[26]

The other illustration of how the individual dissenting will is outlawed is seen in the last story of the book, "Fugitives". John Rodney, a young sculptor, is hired by a priest, Father McCabe, to do a Mother and Child for McCabe's new church. Rodney gets McCabe's cousin, Lucy Delaney, to pose in the nude for him; McCabe discovers this and, after Rodney's sculpture is destroyed by Lucy's two young brothers, Rodney decides to leave Ireland for good. There is no place for the artist in a society where creative originality is frowned on, and sensuousness is equated with sin:

> The wrecking of his studio had broken the last link that bound him to Ireland. "There is no place in Ireland for an artist," he said, "nor yet for a poor man who would live his life in his own way. The rich leave Ireland for pleasure, and the young fellow who would escape from the priest puts it differently. 'Off with me coat,' he says, 'to earn five pounds that'll take me out of Ireland.' " Thank God he was going![27]

"Fugitives" ends with an ironic exposition of the priestly faith in bad art and bad taste, since bad statues are "further removed from perilous nature".[28] By making the political idealist and the creative artist victims of those shoddy values, Moore reveals the shady weaknesses and implacable mediocrity of Ireland as he

[26] *Op. cit.*, p. 221.   [27] *Op. cit.*, p. 233.   [28] *Op. cit.*, p. 245.

knew it. There have been many changes in Irish society (and many for the better) since Moore's day, but *The Untilled Field* is still a monument in the history of the Irish short story. Its influence on Joyce, O'Connor, and O'Faoláin is, I would say, profound. *Dubliners* is, in many ways, like a more sophisticated and more cleverly-organised version of *The Untilled Field*. The two themes of paralysis and escape are common to both books, although Moore is more optimistic insofar as in his stories the characters' desire for escape is frequently realised whereas in *Dubliners* it is usually thwarted. Moore was not being immodest when he claimed that "*The Untilled Field* was a landmark in Anglo-Irish literature, a new departure",[29] although we may disagree with his opinion of the extent of its influence on Synge. In *The Untilled Field*, Moore began to examine a certain sickness at the very heart of Irish society which Joyce later examined at far greater depth. Moore's young sculptor, John Rodney, is remarkably like Joyce's Stephen Daedelus in his deliberate choice of exile, but he lacks Stephen's lofty ambition to forge in the smithy of his soul "the uncreated conscience of my race".[30] Joyce regarded *Dubliners* as "a chapter in the moral history" of Ireland and the Irish people. In this, he was quite right, but *Dubliners* is the second chapter of that moral history. *The Untilled Field* is the first.

3

One of the more regrettable aspects of Moore's career as a short-story writer is that he did not continue in the realistic vein of *The Untilled Field*. The stories in that collection are neatly chiselled, and their critical comments on life in general and Irish life in particular are made in a cleancut, incisive manner which makes a strong and enduring impact on the reader's mind. One would have expected Moore, therefore, to continue in this manner, but instead, he turned his back on the contemporary scene and returned in *A Story-Teller's Holiday* to the colourful primitive world of early Ireland. Even the title indicates a new slackness in Moore and, although *A Story-Teller's Holiday* contains some very

[29] *Op. cit.*, p. xiii.
[30] James Joyce, *Portrait of the Artist as a Young Man*, Harmondsworth (Penguin) 1960, p. 253.

fine stories, the collection as a whole lacks the urgency and passion of *The Untilled Field*. It may be that Moore was reacting against the puritanism which he examined so penetratingly in *The Untilled Field* because the first volume of *A Story-Teller's Holiday* (revised version, 1928) deals almost completely, either in comic or tragic terms, with the theme of temptation. Early Irish Christianity was infinitely less inhibited, and far more expressive, than the modern version, and Moore must have taken great delight in portraying piety enlivened by abandon and in showing how devotion is animated by a vigorous sex-life. As well as that, *A Story-Teller's Holiday* enabled Moore to explore the nature of the *form* of the short story, and this he does with obvious relish and delight in his own experimentation. Ernest Longworth says in the preface that "it is the business of every considerable writer to produce at least one joyous book",[31] and he describes the stories in this book as "spontaneous inventions, with here and there an oddment of folklore, and in the rich, Anglo-Irish idiom they carry a fragrance of newly-upturned earth".[32] *A Story-Teller's Holiday* is experimental in two senses; it is an experiment in the communication of joy, and also in the very nature of the short story itself. Ernest Longworth calls it "a dialogue between the original and the acquired self",[33] but it would be more accurate to describe it as an attempt to show the differences between primitive and sophisticated story-telling. To do this, Moore introduces Alec Trusselby, the *shanachie* or traditional story-teller from Westport, who, at his best, narrates with something approaching the crude, colourful energy that one finds in Old Irish epics such as *Táin Bó Cúailgne*. Alec is the superbly articulate primitive, the Connemara Homer delighting in outrageous events, flamboyant characters and extravagant language spiced with vivid image and metaphor. He is a born story-teller, nothing else seems to matter to him, and he successfully communicates his own profound delight in the world evoked by his primitive imagination. He is, in short, Moore's "original self" against which Moore puts his "acquired self", the educated, sophisticated writer who tells

---

[31] *A Story-Teller's Holiday*, London (Heinemann) 1928, I, p. ix. (This was a two-volume revision of the single volume published in 1918.)

[32] *Ibid.*

[33] *Op. cit.*, p. viii.

stories in a crisp, modern idiom which, if it lacks the expansive
energy of Trusselby's language, has yet an urbane precision and
telling restraint that make it a completely appropriate vehicle for
the sophisticated story-teller. Much of the delight of *A Story-
Teller's Holiday* springs from the balance which Moore creates
between the primitive and the sophisticated. The opening of the
book is marred by dull gossip, slack reminiscence, a conscious
"artiness", and ponderous philosophising, but when he actually
gets down to dealing with the theme of temptation from both the
primitive and sophisticated points of view, we find ourselves, as
if by magic, in a vanished Ireland where the tragedy and the
comedy of temptation are revealed in a rich, lively language.
Moore's monks and nuns form a panorama of bawdy innocents
who might have been created by an Irish Boccaccio. Their
thoughts aspire to heaven, but they are very much of the earth.
They create temptation on earth that they may resist it and therefore gain a higher place in heaven. The question they ask of life
seems to be – if we do not know how far is far enough, then how
can we be expected to know when we are going too far? And
unless we know that, how do we know that we are overcoming
temptation? Such an attitude, with its infinite capacity for showing that amusing and sometimes outrageous double-think which
even today one frequently finds in Irish life, gave Moore, equipped
with a dynamic sense of mischief, ample scope for exploring the
humorous potential of a world in which monks went to bed with
nuns to measure the nuns' power of attraction against their own
power of resistance, and by so doing, to discover precisely the
nature of the evils and the imperfections of this world, and
consequently to aspire more ardently to the perfection of the next.

The second volume of *A Story-Teller's Holiday* deals mainly with
the love-story of Ulick and Soracha, the bastard nobleman and
the beautiful nun who ran away together and, after many adventures, finally came to grief. Moore here sustains the method of
story-telling he used in the first volume, and both Moore and
Trusselby tell different parts of the story, so that when the reader
is beginning to feel that Moore's sophisticated method and idiom
are wearing thin, he is jolted into a new awareness by the sudden
advent of Trusselby's primitive energy. At odd moments
throughout the tale, Moore halts the narrative to discuss it with

Trusselby, so that we never lose sight of the fact that Moore is consciously experimenting with the form of the story.

The love-story itself is skilfully and movingly told, but the most impressive thing in it is the fate of Ulick's old harper, Tadhg O'Dorachy, who, after Ulick and Soracha are dead, lives on, marries a young woman and, after a life completely devoid of love-making, dies watching his wife in her nakedness. Significantly, this part of the story is told by the Westport shanachie, Trusselby: it is Moore's final act of faith in the primitive. As he gaily says to Alec – "You have exceeded me in invention. The Ballinrobe cock is outdone, and the crow is to the Westport rooster!"[34]

One cannot argue that loneliness is consistently portrayed in *A Story-Teller's Holiday*, and yet the most memorable section of that great love-story deals with the loneliness of Tadhg O'Dorachy, the harper, when he is making his journey back to Ireland from Scotland where he had been a slave. Moore describes O'Dorachy's loneliness and hardship at great length, thus preparing us for the pathos of his death. On this journey, we are aware not only of the man's loneliness, but of the loneliness of Ireland itself. Tadhg has only one companion during his suffering – a goose named Maria! Moore, with a wonderfully assured touch, avoids sentimentality in his portrait of the relationship between the harper and the goose. In fact, one of the most moving parts of the story is Tadhg's reaction to Maria's death.

> We were alike and lonely and good to each other. And his grief became so intense that he thought he must die of it, and leaning over the rocks among which he had found a seat he wept upon them for his goose and for himself until he could weep no more. And then he wandered without heed or care whither he was going, not awakening out of the stupor of his grief till the sound of rooks in the branches caught his ear and he said: Wherever there are rooks there is a house, for like poor Maria they are lonely away from the homes of men. And wandering round the rookery he asked himself how it was that so many of the creatures of the earth had given up their freedom to dwell with men. Mayhap, he said, it is

[34] *Op. cit.*, II, p. 223.

because we have souls and they have not; maybe it is our souls that draw them to us.[35]

Yet, despite its many merits, *A Story-Teller's Holiday* is a retrograde step for Moore. It has very little of the formal compactness and concentration of *The Untilled Field*; there are long patches of loose, slack writing, with the result that we occasionally tend to lose interest in the narrative. The lack of contemporary interest is another defect, and while his treatment of the theme of temptation and calculated resistance is extremely amusing, it tends to become rather repetitive. One must conclude that Moore should have continued to cast his cold eye on contemporary Ireland rather than exploring the monkish and nunnish pranks of a much earlier time.

Nevertheless, Moore's importance as a short-story writer is considerable. He has had a deep influence on the Irish short story and, in fact, consciously intended to do this. He considered *The Untilled Field*, he said, as "a book written in the beginning out of no desire of self-expression, but in the hope of furnishing the young Irish of the future with models".[36] This statement, with its emphasis on artistic impersonality and formal experiment, immediately reminds one of Joyce, whose prose is distinguished by precisely these two qualities. Moore had a thematic and formal influence on Joyce. Just as Moore in *The Untilled Field* chose to depict the inhibitions and frustrations of rural Ireland, so Joyce in *Dubliners* chose to describe Catholic Ireland, particularly Catholic Dublin, in all its pious mediocrity, claustrophobic middle-class respectability, garrulous sentimentality, and superstitious religiosity. Though Moore's world is, for the most part, rural, and Joyce's is urban, there are distinct similarities between them. If we compare, for example, Moore's "The Clerk's Quest" with Joyce's "A Little Cloud", we see their portraits of two essentially timid men. Moore's clerk is thus described:

> For thirty years Edward Dempsey had worked low down in the list of clerks in the firm of Quin and Wee. He did his work so well that he seemed born to it. . . He was interested only in his desk . . .
> An obscure, clandestine, taciturn little man occupying in

life only the space necessary to bend over a desk, and whose conical head leaned to one side as if in token of his humility.[37]

Joyce's Little Chandler is similarly timid and anonymous:

> He was called Little Chandler because, though he was but slightly under the average stature, he gave one the idea of being a little man. His hands were white and small and his manners were refined. He took the greatest care of his fair silken hair and moustache, and used perfume discreetly on his handkerchief.[38]

Both these little men suddenly undergo profound changes in their lives and both exchange anonymous timidity for outlandish romanticism. Though, in the end, Moore's character dies of starvation while Joyce's, characteristically, simply stays where he is, one is struck by the formal and thematic similarities between the stories. *Dubliners* shows evidence of far greater craftsmanship and is much more expertly organised, but it would be difficult to deny Joyce's debt to Moore.

Moore was especially aware of the complexity of the perennial Irish problem of exile. In an essay called "Irish Literature", Frank O'Connor writes that it is doubtful "if Irish literature has produced a better short story than 'Home Sickness' ".[39] O'Connor himself wrote constantly about exile in its various forms, and one of Liam O'Flaherty's finest short stories, "Going Into Exile", deals very directly with that bleak Irish fact. "Home Sickness" and "Going Into Exile" are two of the most moving Irish short stories, because exile is as much a part of Irish life as birth and love and death. Both Moore and O'Flaherty fully realised this.

On the whole, Irish prose is more distinguished for its short stories than for its novels (despite *Ulysses*, *Finnegans Wake*, *At-Swim-Two-Birds*, and *Thy Tears Might Cease*). A very distinct Irish short story tradition exists, and today that tradition is being extended by writers such as Brian Friel, Benedict Kiely, Patrick Boyle, John Montague, John McGahern, James Plunkett, Edna O'Brien, and others. It is not at all certain that these writers have read Moore's stories, but it must be conceded that Moore is a

---

[37] *Op. cit.*, p. 147.   [38] *Dubliners*, p. 68.
[39] Unpublished essay (MSS in my possession).

foundation stone of that tradition. As a man, Moore could be arrogant and treacherous; he could sting like a scorpion. But while we may deplore the fact that Moore frequently betrayed his friends through caricature, behaving like some eloquent Iscariot of the Irish literary scene, we must recognise that he remained true to himself as an artist. Letting aside his novels, his contribution to the Irish short story is excellent proof of that.

Graham Hough

GEORGE MOORE AND
THE NOVEL[1]

George Moore was born just over a hundred years ago, and in
just this lapse of time it often happens that a writer has dropped
out of the immediate literary consciousness without yet acquiring
a place in history. This appears to be Moore's present situation.
Though he went on writing until 1928,[2] he lies under the cloud
that obscures the *fin-de-siècle*. But Moore's period (which in this
context means his state of mind as much as his chronological span)
is the period when the English imagination was being profoundly
influenced by the literary experiments of France. It is emerging
from a long imputation of ninetyish triviality: whatever we come
to think of its actual achievement it can only be seen now as an
important chapter of literary history – the introductory chapter,
in fact, to the history that is still being enacted; and with it George
Moore himself is bound to emerge from his obscurity. Perhaps
too there is a feeling that George Moore, the hero of a hundred
anecdotes, is not wholly serious. There have indeed been enough
stories about him, and rather than adding to their number it would
be worth while to inquire why a writer with such a massive
achievement behind him should up to now never quite have made
his mark. Most of the reasons will turn out to be poor ones: but
on the way it should be possible to discover something about what
his achievement really was. For this is by no means easy to
determine.

Of course he himself made it difficult. He issued his work in
limited editions, produced endless revised versions, treated him-

[1] [Reprinted from *Image and Experience: Studies in a Literary Revolution*,
London (Duckworth) Lincoln (University of Nebraska Press) 1960, pp.
00-10.]   [2] [Moore actually wrote up to his death in 1933. Ed.]

self as the author of a sacred scripture, admitting some works to the canon, and casting others out into the apocryphal darkness. All this has made it very hard for the common reader, that final arbiter of literary reputation, to form any clear image of him. In England especially we like our writers to have well-defined personalities that can be recognised in their work, like those of Dr Johnson, Charles Lamb or Bernard Shaw. But George Moore let fall the truth about himself in these words from *Confessions of a Young Man*:

> I came into the world apparently with a nature like a smooth sheet of wax, bearing no impress, but capable of receiving any. Nor am I exaggerating when I say I think I might equally have been a Pharaoh, an ostler, a pimp, an archbishop; and that in the fulfilment of the duties of each a certain measure of success would have been mine.[3]

Moore did as much deliberate self-exhibition as any writer since Rousseau; yet he remains fluid, without outlines, just as he looks in his portrait by Sickert. We can learn something of him by thinking of the diversity of his ambitions: to ride the winner of the National; to paint like Manet; to write like Zola; to be a great lover; to write like Flaubert, Balzac; to be a man of the world; to be an Irish patriot; to write like Landor; to write like Pater. . . . Most of these aspirations represent full-time jobs, quite incompatible with each other. Steeplechasing and painting disappeared pretty early: love and the world hung around rather longer: gradually, writing emerged as the main stream of his life. Merely writing, literature; not founding a school, or disseminating ideas, or influencing society. So that in his old age we see a galaxy of creations – and if we try to look through them to their creator, we see only a ghost; perhaps a mocking, perhaps an embittered, perhaps a contented ghost; surely rather a lonely one, at all events one who has long ago given his flesh and his substance to his works. This waif, this wisp, this near-absurdity that confronts us is what is left of a man whose authentic life was given to the asceticism of the arts. This kind of asceticism has never been much appreciated in English civilisation.

Rather than looking for the man behind the work it would be

[3] *Confessions of a Young Man*, London (Heinemann) 1952, p. 1.

useful to look at the historical situation. What actually were the possibilities for a young novelist in the latter years of the nineteenth century? We must look at France as well as England to explain Moore: but as it happens the answer is the same for both. He could continue the tradition of realism – the rich accumulation of factual particulars, with a strong bias towards social, even sociological interpretation. What had lately become a method and a dogma in France had in an unselfconscious way always been a large component of English fiction in the eighteenth and nineteenth centuries. Or he could begin to develop an almost untried form, the novel of sensibility which neglects the outer definition for the inner, and instead of aiming at objectivity and information, sees the whole through the coloured medium of the author's temperament or through the temperament of some character in the work who becomes for the time being the author's aesthetic representative.

Moore chose realism; very Zolaesque and bedevilled by heredity and environment in *A Mummer's Wife*; infinitely more human and generous in that great novel *Esther Waters*. But a great French novel rather than a great English novel. Although it is about servants' halls, racing stables, lodging houses and pubs, it has little of the smell of English literature. English social portraiture has been strongly tinged with a sort of bourgeois romanticism. Moore complained that the English novelists refused to learn that life is neither jocular nor melodramatic. The world of *Esther Waters* is neither; and it has a sober fidelity to facts as they are that brings it nearer to Flaubert than to the typical English figures, Fielding and Dickens. Fidelity to some of the facts, at least; for English life is really rather jocular; and when it consents to be dramatic at all, it is as likely as not to be melodramatic. But Moore, as an Irishman trained in France, would hardly realise this. He reserves his humour for the practical purpose of annoying his friends, and disdains to put it in his novels, where it could only spoil the texture.

The autobiographies – *Confessions of a Young Man*, *Hail and Farewell*, *Memoirs of my Dead Life* – have probably been most read. Gossip is always popular, and if it is malicious gossip, so much the better. Moore lost many friends by it, and hurt some delicate sensibilities: but there is not really much vice in him, and there is no doubt that he elevated this rather dubious form to the level of a work of art – a work of art whose nature has perhaps not been very well understood. He boasts, for instance, of his amorous successes; in some societies this is fairly normal, but not in ours; and we are at once impelled to ask, Ought he to have said these things? and, irresistibly, I fear, Are they true? The answer to the first question is that by ordinary standards of decency he certainly ought not; the answer to the second is wrapped in mystery: but it rather appears that they were not as true as all that. However, it does not matter much. What he is really doing is writing a sparkling, desultory chronicle whose central figure happens to be called George Moore; and for his other characters he makes free with other actual persons. As a historical record it is probably wrong; as a way of treating one's friends it is certainly shabby; aesthetically it is a success. Since the reader is not implicated, and it is only the social and historical personality of the author that is blamed, perhaps we should anticipate the verdict of posterity and forget these misdemeanours. Some of his victims, anyway, gave as good as they got; Yeats, in the course of a brilliant satirical portrait, revealed that Moore was so unpractical that he had never even discovered how to keep his underpants from slipping down.

This damaging revelation from a fellow-Irishman is satisfactory to lovers of poetic justice, for Moore owed a great deal to Yeats. *Evelyn Innes*, that fine novel which was later expunged from the canon, is dedicated to Yeats; and I have always supposed that the figure of Ulick Dean the musician is partly drawn from him. And when the possibilities of realism seemed to be exhausted, Yeats carried Moore off to Ireland and involved him in the Irish literary movement. Moore was very little of a crusader, but he was intensely sensitive to any breeze that stirred the literary air. For years he had been a Parisian or a Londoner; Ireland, with its sad empty spaces, was almost a new country to him; its moving simplicities recalled the stories of Turgeneff; and association with Yeats recalled another part of his French experience, hitherto unused – what he had learned from the symbolists.

What he had learned from the symbolists was no doubt only a fragment of that mass of poetic theorising at which he must have assisted. Moore's capacity for dealing with ideas was always conspicuously limited. But he had at least absorbed the concept of the work of art as a self-subsistent entity, explicable in its own terms, responsible to its own being, rather than to some reality outside itself. It would seem that the Irish-Yeatsian reactivation of symbolist discussions was the turning-point in Moore's literary life. The stories in *The Untilled Field*, the short novel *The Lake*, are indeed a portrait of Ireland, intimate because he had been born and bred there, fresh because he was a returned traveller: but they are also a movement into an entirely new literary territory – new to Moore and new to English fiction – where the beauty, harmony, and integrity of the words on the page are a more important consideration than their efficacy in representing an outer reality. A transference, in fact, from what Mallarmé had called *l'état brut de la parole* to *l'état essentiel*.

For the most notable aspect of these Irish tales is a linguistic one. Moore claimed that his handling of the Irish idiom in *The Untilled Field* served as a model for J. M. Synge; and this may be true. The tales were written to be translated into Gaelic, as part of a programme for supplying literature in the vernacular. And since they were to appear in another tongue, it was no use to attempt variety, sharp contrasts of style, the setting off of one character's speech against another, all the tricks of "characterisation" that the great Victorian novelists had employed so lavishly. Moore had never been very successful in this (he had no real command of common English speech); and here it would be useless; translation obliterates these distinctions.

Instead he looks for a neutral harmony, a style where all will be in keeping. Among his former friends the painters the greatest crime had been a passage that was out of tone: he now begins to apply the same lesson to literature. What most upsets the harmony in a work of fiction? Natural dialogue, surely. Characters who insist on talking in Cockney, in society slang, in the dialect of an anomalous class or time; whose style refuses to relate itself to that of the author's own reflexions. Some of the more self-conscious novelists had been half aware of this problem already, and kept the servants and the rustics from speaking on that account.

Henry James did not formulate the matter in these terms, but there can be little doubt that it was real to him. The fine intelligence that he requires at the centre of his novels is no doubt there primarily as a moral discriminator: but the restriction of his principal characters to persons of unusual sensibility and perception represents ultimately a stylistic demand – a demand that all shall be in keeping. When the essential dramatis personae make this realistically impossible, he has recourse to a frank convention. The infants in *The Turn of the Screw* talk like Henry James.

All this could hardly have appeared as a problem at any earlier period in the history of fiction. When previous novels had attained the status of works of art it had rarely been in virtue of their texture, and when they had reached the kind of harmony and integrity that a symbolist aesthetic would have approved it had been because of some quite unsymbolist notion of social or literary decorum. After Flaubert, after the aesthetic doctrine of the succeeding generation, the requirement that a novel should not only represent something, but should be something, reaches the level of deliberate awareness. It becomes difficult for the scrupulous novelist to remain content with using language in a mainly referential way, to be satisfied if he points to the right things, no matter by what verbal instrumentality the pointing is done. We are already within sight of the dual allegiance of the early Joyce – the allegiance at once to "realism" and to "beauty". And the great obstacle to the *claritas* and *consonantia* that go to constitute beauty, was the novel's inevitably mixed form. I put this in the past tense, for manifestly the technical situation has now changed: but as the novel stood at the end of the nineteenth century it was always a mixed form – a mixture of narrative for which the author makes himself directly responsible, and dialogue, for which he delegates responsibility to his characters. The situation is not new – it prevails in the epic, as Plato was the first to remark. But the epic was always controlled by a standard of heroic decorum, assimilating all things to its own stylistic level. The novel alone, a bastard new-come form, with no demonstrable noble antecedents, had no such imposed standard of literary manners. And it remained for some refined aesthetic to impose one, to wrestle with the difficulty of a form where the deepest and subtlest considerations, made on the author's own terms, may have to rub shoulders with, or express themselves through, the crudest and most incondite dialect in the mouths of the characters. The narrative and the dramatic methods are always potentially at war. We have glanced at James's solution in passing, and this is not the place even to touch on the varied experiments of the last forty years. Moore's solution is different, and to see it in its developed form we have to look at the last group of novels: *The Brook Kerith* and *Héloïse and Abélard* are the chief.

The first thing one notices about these books is the enormously long unbroken paragraphs, giving a repellently solid appearance to the page. However, they are not what they appear, stretches of unbroken narrative. They are interspersed with conversations, sometimes between two, sometimes between several people: but the indentations and the inverted commas have been suppressed. This is not a mere typographical device, for with a little further investigation we notice that an unbroken rhythm runs through the whole paragraph, narrative and dialogue alike. That is, the peculiarities of individual utterance have been sacrificed to the harmony of the whole. Just the slightest of gestures is made in the direction of naturalism and characterisation; the characters do not all speak alike, there are suggestions of colloquialism and dialect – but only so much as will allow the musical line to run continuously through a whole passage, as it does, for instance, in the enchanting opening of *The Brook Kerith*.

It was at the end of a summer evening, long after his usual bedtime, that Joseph, sitting on his grandmother's knee, heard her tell that Kish having lost his asses sent Saul, his son, to seek them in the land of the Benjamites and the land of Shalisha, whither they might have strayed. But they were not in these lands, Son, she continued, nor in Zulp, whither Saul went afterwards, and being then tired out with looking for them, he said to the servant: We shall do well to forget the asses, lest my father should ask what has become of us. But the servant, being of a mind that Kish would not care to see them without the asses, said to young Saul: Let us go up into yon city, for a great seer lives there and he will be able to put us in the right way to come upon the asses.[4]

Though the date of *The Brook Kerith* is 1916, that is not a modern prose style; far less so than that of *A Mummer's Wife* or the *Confessions* of thirty years before. And *The Brook Kerith* and *Héloïse and*

---

[4] *The Brook Kerith*, London (Heinemann) 1916.

Abélard are remarkably unlike most modern novels. It is natural to begin by talking of George Moore's subject, but one continues by talking of his manner of presentation; for in the later books the manner of presentation has become the subject in a way that the novel previously had hardly known. Of course certain areas of human experience are inevitably represented – in *The Brook Kerith* a notoriously challenging one: the life of Jesus treated as a purely natural and human chronicle. The carpenter's son does not die on the cross, but lives on in hiding. And the tremendous climax comes when, years later, Paul, preaching Christ crucified, is confronted by the still living Jesus. Now if Moore had still been thinking on the lines of the conventional novel the whole plot would have been concentrated on this point; but it is not. It wanders through the Syrian landscape, follows the fortunes of Joseph of Arimathea, lingers among the rival sects and faiths of Palestine. *Héloïse and Abélard* makes the same sort of varied leisurely progress through twelfth-century France. Moore has no historical axe to grind; he shows people behaving as they do behave; alike, in his view, in the first century as in the twelfth, or the nineteenth. There are startling anachronisms, there are digressions and inserted show-pieces, but they hardly matter; the true object of attention throughout is the sustained, slightly soporific texture of the prose, capable of absorbing into itself all the diversities or experience with which it deals.

Moore acknowledged Landor and Pater as his masters, and the writing does remind us of both. But he has given himself a harder task than theirs, for Pater's people do not converse, they only reflect or make set speeches; and Landor's do not act and only occasionally feel. George Moore's triumph is to have combined vividness of presentation with a prose whose rhythm and texture is itself beautiful to contemplate. At this point it will almost certainly be objected that whatever this achievement is worth it has not much to do with the novel. Serious criticism of the novel of late has been so inveterately moralistic that we have been hectored into discussing all works of fiction almost exclusively in terms of just moral discrimination – even if little has been done to show by what standards the justice is assessed. What has been said about Moore's most characteristic achievement has plainly nothing to do with this line of approach. Yet the conscientious contemplator of the novel must give a great deal of weight to this moral approach, not as a moralist himself, for he may make no such pretensions, but because the sphere of the novel is in part the same as that of the moralist – it is the sphere of human conduct, particularly conduct in its social relations. This is true of the novel in a sense that it is not of other forms – of the lyric for instance, whose characteristic material is the moment of apprehension, given, unanalysed, immediate, and therefore morally neutral; of tragedy, whose philosophic analogue is not ethics but metaphysics. There is a general sense in which everything man makes is implicated with his moral experience: but the novel is implicated with it in a special sense as well. And our account of George Moore so far has not touched on this aspect of his work at all, has hardly even suggested that it is there to be touched on. If this were all that is to be said it could well be argued that Moore was an interesting minor experimenter in certain narrative techniques, and that as a novelist he had hardly started.

But of course this is not the whole story about Moore. He tried to choose subjects almost as a decorative painter might try to choose suitable architectural sites for the exhibition of his craft: but whether he would or not, his subjects involved him with life, with an immense variety of human experience. And here we begin to perceive a divergence, a divergence which we might expect, but in Moore's case it is a particularly wide one, between the social personality and the artist. In spite of his exhibitionism, in spite of his faults in taste, in spite, it would appear, of a personal lack of any adequate philosophy, there is in his work a great moral integrity. One doubts if he ever thought about it, and in his best novels it becomes apparent in a singularly effortless and unforced way. We demand a justness of moral perception from the novel, and believe that a good novel could not exist without it any more than a beautiful woman could exist without a backbone. But it is not in virtue of her backbone that she is beautiful; nor is it necessary that she or those who appreciate her beauty should call constant attention to the possession of this indispensable piece of equipment. Moore's work has a moral backbone; it is not in virtue of this that it achieves its peculiar kind of success, but it is nevertheless there, and it is as well to end by insisting on it, for it is in this matter (through the combined skill as caricaturists of himself and his friends) that he is commonly thought to be deficient.

This moral integrity of his work is one that owes much to his early realist training, and, strangely enough, owes something to the insouciance and irresponsibility that puzzles us in his life. Moore has none of the twentieth-century maladies; he does not suffer from anxiety, or a sense of guilt, or the plight of modern man. (I doubt if he knew we were in one.) So his characters are not coloured by any overwhelming emotional tincture of his own. This makes him very unlike most modern novelists: but it also means that he can see people simply as they are. The spectacles through which he looks at the world neither magnify nor diminish, and they are made of uncoloured glass. So that he becomes a superb recorder, quite irrespective of his own sentiments and opinions. We have the paradox that this renegade Catholic, who had rejected all the forms and all the philosophy of the Church, gives in *Evelyn Innes* the superbly understanding study of a woman irresistibly drawn to the religious life; that the callous young arriviste of the *Confessions*, who called pity the vilest of the virtues, can show the grave sympathy for the common lot that runs through *Esther Waters*; that the hero of all the facile sexual success stories should give, in *Héloïse and Abélard*, the infinitely touching story of a love that ends, on this side of the grave, in emptiness and frustration. On the one hand, Moore is the incomparable painter of the world before the deluge: love, sunshine, Paris in the spring; the simple sensual happiness that seems to have vanished from our hag-ridden age; the verbal counterpart of a painting by Renoir. On the other, he can turn a steady gaze on the dramas of asceticism and renunciation. It is hard to believe that *Sister Teresa* and "The Lovers of Orelay" were written by the same man; and it is only possible because the author stands aside; he is not committed; he simply observes and understands. Objective, impersonal comprehension of this kind becomes at its highest pitch a kind of charity. Moore the artist possessed this gift; what he did with it when he was off duty I do not know: but I believe that its presence in his works will be more perceived as the personal legend about him begins to fade.

INDEX